Study Guide to Accompany
POLITICS AND THE AMERICAN FUTURE,
Second Edition

JOHN J. HARRIGAN
Hamline University
St. Paul, Minnesota

Random House   New York

Second Edition

987654321

Copyright © 1987 by Random House, Inc.

ISBN 0-394-36461-9

Manufactured in the United States of America

NOTE TO THE READER

This study guide is a supplement to the text, <u>Politics and the American Future</u>, Second Edition. Its purpose is to help you use the text material in the most effective manner.

This guide is based on a philosophy of learning that seeks to engage you actively in the subject matter and to divide the subject matter into relatively small increments to be mastered. The first item in each chapter asks you to fill in your own substantive summary to the chapter outline rather than simply reading a prepared outline. The second item for each chapter specifies the learning objectives. You can use these in conjunction with the chapter previews and summaries in the text to help you divide the text materials and understand them in an organized way. The third item asks you to write a short identification of the significance of a limited number of important terms, concepts, and names that were used in the chapter. Again, this exercise is designed to engage you actively in the subject matter. The fourth items in each chapter consist of review questions in multiple choice, completion, and true-false format. These are followed by a review exercise that asks you to outline answers to several mastery questions. Correct responses to the multiple choice, true-false, and completion test items are provided toward the last page of each chapter.

Most chapters also contain a "Beyond the Text" exercise. Again, based on an active learning philosophy, these exercises are designed to accomplish two goals. First, they should help you apply some principles discussed in the chapters to real life contemporary situations. Second, they seek to familiarize you with some important resources for interpreting and understanding American politics. By applying textbook principles to real situations and by learning about political science resources, these "Beyond the Text" exercises should give you more tools and the confidence to explore subjects on your own.

Many exciting things happen each year in the American political system. I hope this text and this study guide help to provide a meaningful context for understanding those events and seeing what makes American politics so fascinating.

John J. Harrigan
Hamline University
St. Paul, Minnesota

CONTENTS

Chapter 1

THE CHALLENGE OF THE
AMERICAN FUTURE

CHAPTER OUTLINE

Write a one-sentence summary of the materials found under each of the headings and subheadings in the text:

LEARNING OBJECTIVES

After reading Chapter 1 and doing the exercises in this study guide, you should be able to:

1. Explain the connection between your own future and that of American society.
2. Understand the challenges of the American future and why the American government must formulate effective policies to meet those challenges.
3. List and explain some of the doubts about government's ability to cope with various challenges over the next three decades.
4. Discuss the impact of the electronic media revolution and the litigation explosion as sea changes on the American political system.
5. Summarize the text's main emphases.

IDENTIFICATION ITEMS

Write out a one- or two-sentence identification that gives the significance of the following terms or names to this chapter:

Bill of Rights
Policy issues and personal impact
Energy-environment challenges
Inflation
Stagflation
Sea change
Litigation explosion
Electronic media revolution
Nuclear proliferation
James Sundquist

Megatrends
Civil liberties
Habeus corpus
Nuclear club
Watergate
Pentagon Papers
Pornography
Survivalism
Lester Thurow
Alexis de Tocqueville

REVIEW QUESTIONS

Multiple Choice Questions

1. At present consumption rates, the world's oil and natural gas reserves will be exhausted in:
   a. 30 years
   b. 50 years
   c. 300 years
   d. 75 years

2. The United States has:
   a. the world's highest per capita income
   b. the world's lowest infant mortality rate
   c. both a and b
   d. none of the above

3. By 1970, the proportion of people below the official poverty line was:
   a. one in five
   b. one in eight
   c. one in two
   d. one in ten

4. In a growing national economy, the individual's share of the economic pie:
   a. can become larger over time
   b. can become larger over time only at the expense of others
   c. both a and b
   d. none of the above

5. Japanese-Americans were forced into internment camps during:
   a. World War I
   b. the Korean War
   c. World War II
   d. the Vietnam War

6. Which of the following factors could lead to a nuclear war?
   a. nuclear proliferation
   b. terrorism
   c. an accident/false alarm
   d. all of the above

7. Which of the following countries is not a member of the nuclear club? ·
   a. China
   b. France
   c. Japan
   d. all of the above are members

2

8. In which of the following governmental institutions do citizens have the greatest degree of confidence?
   a. Congress
   b. Supreme Court
   c. presidency
   d. military

9. According to economist Lester Thurow, the "root cause" of America's economic problems is:
   a. interest-group representation
   b. poor leadership
   c. governmental complexity
   d. Soviet competition

10. Political reform may be limited by:
    a. a poorly functioning government
    b. unintended consequences of reform
    c. both a and b
    d. neither a nor b

11. The kinds of public services available in the future are directly related to the issues of:
    a. the world's supply of oil and natural gas
    b. the world's population
    c. governmental taxing/spending policies
    d. the world's health

12. The two most likely energy alternatives to gas and oil are:
    a. solar and geothermal energy
    b. nuclear power and coal
    c. tidal/wind power
    d. none of the above

13. The growth of the American middle class was chiefly due to:
    a. the continuing growth of the economy
    b. the end of poverty in America
    c. the small number of immigrants over the last thirty years
    d. all of the above

14. At one time or the other, civil liberties/rights have been denied to:
    a. Japanese-Americans
    b. black Americans
    c. American Indians
    d. all of the above

15. In New York Times v. US, the Supreme Court ruled that:
    a. the secret Pentagon Papers could not be published
    b. the secret Pentagon Papers could be published, but only after a waiting period of six months
    c. the secret Pentagon Papers could be published without delay
    d. the secret Pentagon Papers should not have been written in the first place

16. In a nuclear war involving both Soviet and American cities, the estimated total of people killed in both countries is:
    a. 250 million
    b. 350 million
    c. 125 million
    d. 110 million

17. From 1966 to 1984, public confidence has usually been consistently lowest for which American political institution?
    a. executive branch
    b. the Supreme Court
    c. the military
    d. Congress

3

18. Which of the following was not cited as evidence of a litigation explosion in America today?
    a. the growth of civil suits filed in courts
    b. the growth in the number of lawyers
    c. the growing tendency to turn to the courts to confront social and political issues
    d. the growing number of prisoners in American prisons

19. The public and media most often focus on:
    a. issues
    b. personalities
    c. political tradeoffs
    d. historical background of issues

20. The text stresses that this book is mainly:
    a. a justification for the status quo
    b. a rebuke of the American political system
    c. an argument for both preservation and systemic change
    d. all of the above

Completion Questions

1. Increasing oil and natural gas production and not limiting economic growth is the energy solution offered by political _____.

2. While the United States rate of savings and investment _____ in the 1970s and early 1980s, debt has _____.

3. Economic stagnation and inflation, when combined, is termed _____.

4. The Pentagon Papers were secret government papers outlining a history of the decision-making process of _____.

5. The individual who gave the Pentagon Papers to The New York Times was _____.

6. The number of Americans who could be killed in a nuclear war involving attacks on cities is about _____ million.

7. Nations already suspected of possessing nuclear weapons are _____ and _____.

8. In the 1980 election, Ronald Reagan defeated President _____.

9. The _____ have transformed the way in which we finance and conduct elections, have brought the daily trauma of international troubles into our living room, and have contributed to a fundamental alteration in the relationship between the president, the Congress, and the people.

10. In 1835, _____ noted that in America most major political issues end up being contested in the courts.

True-False Questions

T   F   1. The individual American's well-being is closely linked to the nation's welfare.

T   F   2. Since 1970, the United States' economy has been expanding even faster than in the previous decades.

T   F   3. Generally, there is a consensus on how the national economy should be managed.

T   F   4. The litigation explosion has had a profound effect on the presidency and Congress as well as on the federal courts.

T   F   5. Some military leaders argue that a nuclear war is survivable.

T   F   6. Public confidence in governmental institutions is higher in the 1980s than it was in the 1960s.

T   F   7. Charles Schultze believes in changing our system of governmental regulation of the economy.

T   F   8. The President's Commission for a National Agenda for the 1980s concluded that priorities in the 1980s will be increasingly difficult to establish.

T   F   9. Litigation was not an important channel for social change in the 1960s and 1970s; it only became important in the 1980s.

T   F 10. President Reagan's 1981 legislative success was mainly due to the force of his personality.

Mastery Questions

Outline a response to each of the following:

1. Review the four policy issues that will have a personal impact upon the American citizen's future.

2. Review the Pentagon Papers case, explaining why the papers were important and what the Supreme Court ruling entailed.

3. Describe the kind of destruction that would result from a full-scale nuclear war between the United States and the Soviet Union.

4. What are the disadvantages of thinking about the leadership problem in terms of personalities?

5. Discuss the concept of sea changes in American politics. In what respects are the litigation explosion and the electronic media revolution sea changes?

ANSWERS TO REVIEW QUESTIONS (WITH PAGE NUMBERS)

Multiple Choice

1.	a, p. 3	11.	c, p. 2	
2.	d, p. 4	12.	b, p. 3	
3.	b, p. 4	13.	a, p. 4	
4.	a, p. 4	14.	d, p. 8	
5.	c, p. 5	15.	c, p. 7	
6.	d, p. 10	16.	a, p. 9	
7.	c, p. 10	17.	d, p. 11	
8.	b, p. 11	18.	d, p. 13	
9.	a, p. 10	19.	b, p. 15	
10.	c, p. 16	20.	c, p. 17	

Completion

1. conservatives, p. 3
2. declined, increased, p. 4
3. stagflation, p. 5
4. the Vietnam War, p. 6
5. Daniel Ellsberg, p. 6
6. 140, p. 9
7. Israel, S. Africa p. 10
8. Carter, p. 11
9. electronic media, p. 13
10. Alexis de Tocqueville, p. 13

True-False

1.	T, p. 2	6.	F, p. 11
2.	F, p. 4	7.	T, p. 10
3.	F, p. 5	8.	T, p. 12
4.	T, p. 14	9.	F, p. 14
5.	T, p. 9	10.	F, p. 15

Chapter 2

CONSTITUTIONAL CONSTRAINTS AND THE
AMERICAN FUTURE

CHAPTER OUTLINE

Write a one-sentence summary of the materials found under each of the headings and subheadings in the text.

LEARNING OBJECTIVES

After reading Chapter 2 and doing the exercises in this study guide, you should be able to:

1. Explain the relative weaknesses of the Articles of Confederation vis-a-vis the strengths of the Constitution.
2. Elaborate upon the fundamental compromises and/or plans which were agreed to by the Founding Fathers at the Constitutional Convention.

3. Review the basic assumptions of the Beard thesis and the critical arguments against the thesis.
4. Discuss the concept of limited government derived from European philosophers and describe how the following constitutional provisions are relevant to limited government: federalism, the Bill of Rights, separation of powers, checks and balances.
5. Describe the procedures for amending the Constitution and cite examples of specific amendments.
6. Discuss the relationship between litigation and the Constitution.

IDENTIFICATION ITEMS

Write out a one- or two-sentence identification that gives the significance of the following terms or names to this chapter:

James Madison
Alexander Hamilton
Charles Beard
Baron de Montesquieu
George Washington
Thomas Jefferson
Virginia Plan
Civil liberties
Judicial review
Great (Connecticut) Compromise
National supremacy clause
Federalism
Separation of powers
Madisonian model
Balanced budget amendment proposal
Fundamental law
Change through interpretation
Spirit of the Laws
Federalist Papers
Treatise on Civil Government

An Economic Interpretation
   of the Constitution
Daniel Shays
John Jay
John Locke
John Adams
Benjamin Franklin
New Jersey Plan
Enumerated powers
Delegated powers
Reserved powers
Three-fifths compromise
Necessary-and-proper clause
Civil liberties
Checks and balances
Limited government
ERA
Statutory law
Fourteenth Amendment
Articles of Confederation

REVIEW QUESTIONS

Multiple Choice Questions

1. The "father" of the Constitution was:
   a. Thomas Jefferson
   b. Alexander Hamilton
   c. George Washington
   d. James Madison

2. How many delegates actually attended the Constitutional Convention?
   a. 74
   b. 55
   c. 39
   d. 47

3. Which of the following was not wanted by the conservatives at the Constitutional Convention?
   a. protection of U.S. securities
   b. protection of investments in western lands
   c. sovereignty of state legislatures
   d. all of the above were wanted by the conservatives

4. Which of the following powers was denied to Congress under the Articles of Confederation?
   a. the power to regulate commerce
   b. the power to raise money through taxation
   c. both a and b
   d. the power to pass laws

5. The state which had the most extreme inflationary environment during the period of the Articles of Confederation was probably:
   a. Rhode Island
   b. Massachusetts
   c. Virginia
   d. Georgia

6. Which of the following leaders did not attend the Constitutional Convention?
   a. John Adams
   b. Thomas Jefferson
   c. John Hancock
   d. None of these attended

7. If a state has two senators and six representatives, its total number of electoral votes will be:
   a. eight
   b. six
   c. two
   d. four

8. If a state in the South had 100,000 slaves in its population during the period before slavery was eradicated, how many slaves would be counted for determining that state's representation in the House of Representatives?
   a. 50,000
   b. 60,000
   c. 80,000
   d. 100,000

9. Anti-Federalists objected to the Constitution because the document:
   a. slighted the judicial branch
   b. lacked a Bill of Rights
   c. had been drafted in total secrecy
   d. could be ratified by less than a unanimous vote of the states

10. "Ambition must be made to counteract ambition" is a famous statement by:
    a. Thomas Jefferson in the Declaration of Independence
    b. James Madison in The Federalist Papers
    c. Alexander Hamilton in the Articles of Confederation
    d. Benjamin Franklin in the Constitution

11. Which political philosopher and/or statesman is associated with the separation of powers concept?
    a. Locke
    b. Jefferson
    c. Rousseau
    d. Montesquieu

12. The Constitution has contributed to litigation as a means of resolving political disputes primarily because of the principle of:
    a. judicial review
    b. federalism
    c. limited government
    d. separation of powers

13. According to John Locke, natural rights:
    a. were granted to the people by the government
    b. could be withdrawn from the people without their consent under certain circumstances
    c. were granted to people by the Constitution's Bill of Rights and could be withdrawn only by Congress
    d. were superior to governmental rights and thus could not be withdrawn by governments

14. The statement "The government which governs best governs least" is attributed to:
    a. Thomas Paine
    b. Thomas Jefferson
    c. John Locke
    d. Alexander Hamilton

15. Of the over 5,000 proposals for constitutional amendments that have been introduced in Congress since 1787, how many have been duly initiated and ratified?
    a. 100 initiated; 32 ratified
    b. 15 initiated; 10 ratified
    c. 26 initiated; 19 ratified
    d. none of the above is correct

16. The Equal Rights amendment proposal fell how many states short of ratification?
    a. thirteen
    b. six
    c. three
    d. twenty-five

17. Reapportionment, desegregation, and affirmative action Supreme Court rulings have been based upon which amendment to the U.S. Constitution:
    a. Fourteenth
    b. First
    c. Sixth
    d. Nineteenth

18. Which of the following is a problem dealing with the "adequacy of the Constitution"?
    a. the ability of government to respond swiftly to problems
    b. the rationale for existing state boundaries
    c. both a and b
    d. none of the above

19. In considering new forms for the United States, the Center for the Study of Democratic Institutions has proposed:
    a. nine "nations," keeping existing state boundaries intact
    b. twenty republics, emphasizing regional boundaries
    c. eliminating the states and having only a single national government
    d. all of the above

20. Currently, how many employees work in the federal government?
    a. 1.9 million
    b. 5.3 million
    c. 4.6 million
    d. 2.8 million

Completion Questions

1. An armed debtors' rebellion that occurred in Massachusetts in 1786 was dubbed _____.

2. According to the text, roughly _____ percent of the American people had backed separation from England during the Revolution.

3. Three prominent radicals at the time of the Articles of Confederation were Sam Adams, _____, and _____.

4. Another name for the "firm league of friendship" was the _____.

5. The plan which provided for unicameral legislature, with an equal number of members from each state, was the _____ plan.

6. Two other names for the necessary-and-proper clause of Article I, Section 8 of the Constitution are the _____ or the _____.

7. The three authors of The Federalist Papers were _____, _____, and _____.

8. Constitutional scholars oppose a balanced budget amendment because it blurs the distinction between _____ and _____ law.

9. The power to judge whether the acts of other governmental institutions are constitutional is termed _____.

10. An Economic Interpretation of the Constitution by _____ argued that the founders had drafted the Constitution more to protect their economic self-interest than to create a democratic government.

True-False Questions

T   F   1. In 1787, British soldiers continued to occupy American soil.

T   F   2. Apparently, Madison extensively adopted the governmental structures of ancient Greece and Rome in creating the American model of government.

T   F   3. Under the Articles of Confederation, members of Congress could not serve more than three one-year terms in any six-year period.

T   F   4. Probably the state most controlled by the debtor classes was Massachusetts.

T   F   5. Small farmers were heavily represented by the convention delegates in 1787.

T   F   6. The Founding Fathers considered the legislative branch to be the "least dangerous branch of government."

T   F   7. Within ten months of submission, twelve of the thirteen states had ratified the new Constitution.

T   F   8. The natural rights under Locke's contract theory of government included those of life, liberty, and property.

T   F   9. The concept of five branches of government would include the Supreme Court, Congress, the presidency, presidential appointees, and the bureaucracy.

T   F   10. It could be argued that the Constitution means what five Supreme Court justices say it means.

Mastery Questions

Outline a response to each of the following:

1. Describe some of the major governmental weaknesses and list three policy accomplishments under the Articles of Confederation.

2. What specifically constituted the "series of adverse developments in the 1780s" which collectively accelerated the movement toward a constitutional convention?

3. Describe the general background--social, political, economic--of the framers of the Constitution. Does this background help to explain the Beard thesis? Why or why not? Be sure to review the Beard thesis in detail. Summarize the critical reactions to the Beard thesis.

4. Review the significance of the following: Connecticut Compromise, three-fifths compromise, national supremacy clause, judicial review.

5. Explain the Madisonian model of government. What are its principal strengths and weaknesses?

6. Discuss the relevance of the Constitution to today's controversy over the litigation explosion.

ANSWERS TO QUESTIONS (WITH PAGE NUMBERS)

Multiple Choice

		Completion
1. d, p. 23	11. d, p. 34	1. Shays's Rebellion, p. 22
2. b, p. 23	12. a, p. 43	2. forty, p. 23
3. c, p. 23	13. d, p. 37	3. Patrick Henry, Thomas Paine, p. 23
4. c, p. 24	14. a, p. 37	4. Articles of Confederation, p. 24
5. a, p. 24	15. d, p. 38	5. New Jersey Plan, p. 28
6. d, p. 25	16. c, p. 38	6. elastic, implied powers, p. 29
7. a, p. 30	17. a, p. 41	7. Hamilton, Jay, Madison, p. 33
8. b, p. 32	18. c, p. 43	8. fundamental-statutory, p. 40
9. b, p. 33	19. b, p. 43	9. judicial review, p. 39
10. b, p. 34	20. d, p. 41	10. Charles Beard, p. 26

True-False

1. T, p. 21   6. F, p. 31
2. F, p. 22   7. F, p. 33
3. T, p. 24   8. T, p. 36
4. F, p. 24   9. T, p. 41
5. F, p. 26   10. T, p. 42

BEYOND THE TEXT: Should we have a new Constitutional Convention?

To sharpen your insights into the framing of the Constitution in 1787 and today's controversy over the issue of calling for a convention to draft a balanced budget amendment proposal, construct a scenario for a balanced budget amendment convention today. In your scenario, make note of the following "facts" of the 1787 convention that are generally considered to have facilitated its success. Could these facts be replicated in a convention held today? If so, what would be their likely consequences for the kinds of proposals coming out of the convention? That is, would they be likely to facilitate or impede a fair and successful Constitution?

1. The 1787 convention met behind closed doors, closed to the press, closed to outside observers, and free from today's practice of leaking information to reporters. Could this be the case today?

2. Many of the most important leaders of the 1787 convention had a deep understanding of political philosophy and distinguished practical political experience. Can you name anybody on the national scene today with comparable accomplishments to lead a constitutional convention?

3. The 1787 convention aborted its defined task of drafting amendments to the Articles of Confederation and instead wrote a brand new constitution. Could a convention today be limited to drafting a single amendment?

4. If Charles Beard is correct, the overwhelming majority of the people were not represented at 1787 convention, and delegates shared some common economic interests that enabled them to overcome their regional and political differences. Could this be true of a convention today? If it were true, how much trust would you place in such a convention to represent your interests?

5. The 1787 convention concerned itself primarily with the broad outline of governmental structure and political rights, not the narrow details of government policy. It was concerned more with establishing the fundamental law than with legislating statutory law. Would this be true of a convention dedicated to balancing the federal budget?

Chapter 3

FEDERALISM AND THE
INTERGOVERNMENTAL LABYRINTH

CHAPTER OUTLINE

Write a one-sentence summary of the materials found under each of the headings and subheadings in the text: .

LEARNING OBJECTIVES

After reading Chapter 3 and doing the exercises in this study guide, you should be able to:

1. List and explain both the merits and demerits of the intergovernmental system.
2. Outline the basic features of federalism, noting the differences between the dual and cooperative types.
3. Explain the grants-in-aid system along with categorical, block, and revenue-sharing grants.
4. Describe fully the role of regionalism in the intergovernmental system, with particular attention to the Sunbelt-Frostbelt and Sagebrush Rebellion examples.
5. Elaborate on the salient features of President Reagan's New Federalism.

IDENTIFICATION ITEMS

Write out a one- or two-sentence identification that gives the significance of the following terms or names to this chapter:

Federalism
Confederation
Equal-protection clause
National supremacy clause
Fourteenth Amendment
Privileges-and-immunities clause
Project grant
Block grant
Open-ended reimbursement
Reserved powers
Necessary-and-proper clause
Dual federalism
Layer-cake federalism
Loose constructionist
McCulloch v. Maryland
Brown v. Board of Education
Interstate compact
Port Authority of New York and New Jersey
Sagebrush Rebellion
Sunbelt
Frostbelt
Urban enterprise zone
Unitary government

Commerce clause
Formula grant
Due-process clause
Rendition clause
Full-faith-and-credit clause
Categorical grant
General revenue sharing
Delegated (or enumerated) powers
Concurrent powers
Implied powers
Cooperative federalism
Marble-cake federalism
Strict constructionist
Plessy v. Ferguson
Roe v. Wade
Regionalism
UDAG
CDBG
New Federalism
Devolution
Great Swap
AFDC

REVIEW QUESTIONS

Multiple Choice Questions

1. The government of England is a/an:
   a. federal government
   b. unitary government
   c. confederation
   d. anarchy

15

2. The power to tax is an example of a:
   a. concurrent power
   b. enumerated power
   c. delegated power
   d. reserved power

3. John Marshall's famous statement that the power to tax is the power to destroy is found in:
   a. Marbury v. Madison
   b. Plessy v. Ferguson
   c. McCulloch v. Maryland
   d. Roe v. Wade

4. The 1964 Civil Rights Act was specifically related to the:
   a. due-process clause
   b. taxing power
   c. equal-protection clause
   d. commerce clause

5. Roe v. Wade dealt with the issue of:
   a. abortion
   b. segregation
   c. federal grants
   d. national supremacy

6. The Interstate Highway Program is an example of a:
   a. general revenue sharing
   b. block grant
   c. categorical grant
   d. open-ended reimbursement

7. The UDAG is a/an:
   a. project grant
   b. block grant
   c. formula grant
   d. open-ended reimbursement

8. Toy governments:
   a. receive no revenue-sharing funds
   b. number only a few hundred nationally
   c. both a and b
   d. none of the above

9. According to the text, Congress, in authorizing CDBGs in 1977 and 1980:
   a. gave extra weight to communities with high per-capita tax burdens
   b. gave extra weight to communities with population growth rates below the national average
   c. both a and b
   d. none of the above

10. The marble-cake brand of federalism can also be called:
    a. cooperative federalism
    b. dual federalism
    c. layer-cake federalism
    d. complex federalism

11. The clause that requires governors to return fugitives to states from which they fled is:
    a. full faith and credit
    b. privileges and immunities
    c. rendition
    d. due process

12. The Port Authority of New York and New Jersey exemplifies:
    a. revenue sharing
    b. home rule
    c. regionalism
    d. interstate compact

13. The region of the nation that experienced the largest percentage of population growth from 1975 to 1983 was the:
    a. Northeast
    b. West
    c. South
    d. North Central

14. Which of the following is an issue in the Sagebrush Rebellion?
    a. land
    b. energy
    c. water
    d. all of the above

15. Which of the following did the Land Policy and Management Act of 1976 not do?
    a. prohibit overgrazing of federal lands
    b. replace ten-year leases with five-year leases
    c. require environmental impact statements
    d. the act did all of the above

16. Which of the following states have placed severance taxes on energy resources?
    a. Montana
    b. Wyoming
    c. Alaska
    d. all of the above

17. Under Reagan's Great Swap proposal, which specific program(s) was/were to be turned over to the states?
    a. AFDC
    b. Food Stamps
    c. Medicaid
    d. a and b, but not c

18. New Federalism is essentially a conflict:
    a. between states and the federal government
    b. between Democrats and Republicans
    c. between conservative and liberal groups
    d. between North and South

19. Which is a strength of the intergovernmental system?
    a. innovation
    b. adaptability
    c. multiple access points
    d. all of the above

20. American federalism historically enabled the states to have a poor record on:
    a. the environment
    b. civil liberties
    c. both a and b
    d. none of the above

Completion Questions

1. There are over _____ governments in America.

2. Layer-cake federalism can also be called _____ federalism.

3. The equal-protection clause is associated with the _____ Amendment to the Constitution.

4. Categorical grants take two forms: _____ grants or _____ grants.

5. The CDBG grant program was aimed at aiding _____.

6. Five basic forms of local government are _____, _____, _____, _____, and _____.

7. The region of the nation which experienced the smallest growth in nonagricultural employment between 1975 and the mid-1980s was the _____ region.

8. _____ West interests wish to use the land for multiple uses.

9. The keynote of President Reagan's New Federalism was the concept of _____.

10. Under Reagan's New Federalism proposals, _____ _____ _____ were intended to reinvigorate city neighborhoods through tax incentives.

True-False Questions

T   F   1. Both the words _federal_ and _federalism_ appear several times in the United States Constitution.

T   F   2. Strict construction refers to interpreting the Constitution to meet the changing needs of the times.

T   F   3. _Plessy_ v. _Ferguson_ established the separate but equal doctrine.

T   F   4. Block grants have fewer federal guidelines or restrictions than categorical grants.

T   F   5. The revenue-sharing program currently funds both state and local government.

T   F   6. Home rule signifies greater state independence from federal controls.

T   F   7. The Sagebrush Rebellion was initiated by the state of Nevada.

T   F   8. Most of the nation's energy-producing areas are located in the West.

T   F   9. The West is water poor but energy rich.

T   F   10. Reagan's New Federalism is basically a politically neutral proposal.

Mastery Questions

Outline a response to each of the following:

1. Why does the text compare federalism to Rubik's Cube?

2. Explain how a child-protection worker exemplifies federalism in action.

18

3. Review the central issues and constitutional significance of <u>McCulloch</u> v. <u>Maryland</u> and <u>Brown</u> v. <u>Board of Education</u>.

4. Explain how the federal income tax and the system of grants-in-aid have promoted federal supremacy.

5. Why does Congress prefer formula grants to project grants?

6. Why and how is the federal grants-in-aid program neither simple nor unbiased?

7. Specify why government programs tend toward functional specialization.

8. Explain how the rise of the Sunbelt and the West in the national political economy has complicated the system of federalism.

9. List and summarize the basic strengths and weaknesses of the intergovernmental system.

ANSWERS TO REVIEW QUESTIONS (WITH PAGE NUMBERS)

Multiple Choice

1. b, p. 51   11. c, p. 65
2. a, p. 54   12. d, p. 66
3. c, p. 56   13. b, p. 67
4. d, p. 57   14. d, p. 67
5. a, p. 58   15. b, p. 68
6. c, p. 59   16. d, p. 69
7. a, p. 59   17. d, p. 72
8. d, p. 62   18. c, p. 73
9. b, p. 63   19. d, p. 74
10. a, p. 63   20. c, p. 75

Completion

1. 80,000, p. 53
2. dual, p. 54
3. Fourteenth, p. 56
4. project, formula, p. 59
5. cities or urban areas, p. 59
6. municipalities, towns, counties, special districts, school districts, p. 65
7. North Central, p. 67
8. New, p. 69
9. devolution, p. 71
10. urban enterprise zones, p. 72

True-False

1. F, p. 54   6. F, p. 64
2. F, p. 55   7. T, p. 66
3. T, p. 56   8. T, p. 69
4. T, p. 60   9. T, p. 70
5. F, p. 60   10. F, p. 73

Chapter 4

POLITICAL BELIEFS, THE MEDIA,
AND PUBLIC POLICY

CHAPTER OUTLINE

Write a one-sentence summary of the materials found under each of the headings and subheadings in the text.

LEARNING OBJECTIVES

After reading Chapter 4 and doing the exercises in this study guide, you should be able to:

1. Understand what political beliefs are and how they influence public policy.
2. Explain why Americans are not extreme ideologues and why there was a decline in confidence in the political system in the 1970s.
3. Elaborate upon the dynamics of the political socialization process, noting the effects of the family, schools, peer groups, and the media upon the formation and evolution of public opinion.
4. Describe the three fundamental political roles of the media.
5. List and summarize basic American beliefs (and contradictions) regarding the economy, foreign and defense policy, and democratic principles.

IDENTIFICATION ITEMS

Write out a one- or two-sentence identification that gives the significance of the following terms or names to this chapter:

Legitimacy
Public opinion
Survey research
National Opinion Research Center
Ideological spectrum
Neoconservative
Neoliberal
Ideologue
Nature-of-the-times voter
Issue inconsistency
Crisis of confidence theory
Performance dissatisfaction theory
Affective socialization
Electronic media
Print media
Middle-ring media
FCC
Structural bias
Stephen Hess
Political culture

Gallup Poll
Center for Political Studies
Literary Digest
Conservative
Liberal
Intensity problem
Group benefits voter
No-issue-content voter
Issue constraints
Political socialization
Cognitive socialization
Agents of socialization
Media
Inner-ring media
Outer-ring media
Two-step communication process
Fairness Doctrine
Samuel Stoufer
Walter Lippman

REVIEW QUESTIONS

Multiple Choice Questions

1. Legitimacy is based upon:
    a. a broad public acceptance of the government's role
    b. an overwhelming public opinion
    c. both a and b are correct
    d. imposition of government rule by military force

2. The phrase "people form pictures inside their heads" is associated with:
   a. George Gallup
   b. Walter Lippman
   c. Harry Truman
   d. Phillip Converse

3. The set of beliefs and attitudes that people hold about particular political issues is termed:
   a. political culture
   b. legitimacy
   c. public opinion
   d. consensus

4. For national surveys, polling organizations can accurately (within a 4 percent margin of error) reflect public opinion with a sample as small as:
   a. 3,000 people
   b. 2,000 people
   c. 500 people
   d. 1,500 people

5. The Literary Digest in 1936:
   a. correctly predicted FDR's presidential election victory
   b. employed a sample of only 1,000 people
   c. used a highly effective sampling technique
   d. made a wrong prediction for the presidential election

6. Which of the following is true?
   a. Basic U.S. consensual values produce nondecisions.
   b. No American president in the twentieth century has been reelected during an economic recession.
   c. There is little direct relationship between public opinion and congressional voting on most issues.
   d. All of the above are true.

7. According to Miller and Stokes, public opinion affected congressional voting most on the issue of:
   a. foreign policy
   b. civil rights
   c. capital punishment
   d. war and peace

8. On which issue do legislators find public opinion to be highly emotional?
   a. gun control
   b. abortion
   c. both a and b
   d. the environment

9. An ideology located on the "right" side of the political spectrum is:
   a. liberal
   b. conservative
   c. communist
   d. socialist

10. Voters who vote for a candidate mainly on good looks would fall into the category of:
    a. nature-of-the-times voter
    b. ideologue
    c. group benefits voter
    d. no-issue-content voter

11. Scammon and Wattenberg believe:
    a. the liberal era has ended
    b. public opinion will remain hawkish on foreign policy
    c. both a and b are true
    d. both a and b are false

12. A <u>complete</u> conservative would be conservative on:
    a. economics
    b. foreign policy
    c. social policy
    d. all of the above

13. Which is true?
    a. Some recent studies indicate that voters are becoming more ideologically consistent.
    b. Highly educated citizens are less issue-consistent than poorly educated citizens.
    c. Both a and b are true.
    d. Both a and b are false.

14. The earliest socialization responses are usually:
    a. cognitive
    b. negative
    c. affective
    d. all of the above

15. In the teenage years, the socialization agent with the greatest influence is the:
    a. peer group
    b. school
    c. family
    d. media

16. The school curriculum:
    a. has a major impact upon the child's knowledge of the political system
    b. has a bigger impact on white children than on children of racial minorities
    c. both a and b are true
    d. both a and b are false

17. Studies show that college moves students toward a more:
    a. conservative orientation
    b. socialist orientation
    c. liberal orientation
    d. radical orientation

18. According to Stephen Hess, newspapers such as the <u>Los Angeles Times</u> or the <u>Chicago Tribune</u> would be located in which level of the news media hierarchy?
    a. inner ring
    b. middle ring
    c. outer ring
    d. top strata

19. Most newspapers appear to be:
    a. liberal
    b. conservative
    c. middle of the road
    d. communist

20. Regarding the economic beliefs of Americans:
    a. Upper-income people are more likely than low-income people to support government intervention in the economy.
    b. Americans are politically neutral toward welfare.
    c. There is widespread support for Medicare and Social Security.
    d. There is growing support for socialism as opposed to capitalism.

Completion Questions

1. _____ means "that the overwhelming majority of citizens freely accept the government's right to make basic political decisions."

2. The two best-known commercial polls are the _____ and the _____.

3. NORC is located at the University of _____.

4. According to a 1981 poll, _____ percent of the public favors handgun licenses.

5. _____ ideology supports governmental intervention in the economy.

6. A union member voter who voted for pro-labor Democratic candidates could be classified as a _____ voter.

7. The process by which citizens acquire political knowledge is _____.

8. The family's strongest impact upon the child is his or her _____ _____ orientation.

9. Americans get most of their political information from _____.

10. The emergence of the environmental movement in the early 1970s illustrates the media's _____ _____ role.

True-False Questions

T   F   1. Increasingly, Americans no longer accept the legitimacy of their government.

T   F   2. Public opinion is an expression of the political culture.

T   F   3. The Gallup Poll in 1948 predicted a defeat for President Truman.

T   F   4. Basically, the public's level of political information has been low over the last three decades.

T   F   5. The majority of Americans today are either liberal or extreme liberals.

T   F   6. Public opinion is more conservative in the 1980s than it was in the 1960s.

T   F   7. Issue inconsistency is common among the American people.

T   F   8. Political participation is more likely for upper-class than for lower-class families.

T   F   9. The two-step communication process is equally applicable to both highly educated and poorly educated individuals.

T   F   10. Inner-ring media stories are most likely to reach the president's attention.

Mastery Questions

Outline a response to each of the following:

1. List and discuss the three conditions under which public policy is most likely to follow public opinion. What is meant by the intensity problem in public opinion?

2. Outline the differences between liberalism and conservativism. How do the concepts of neoliberalism and neoconservativism fit into this classification?

3. Describe the four classifications of voters on the basis of their attitudes toward issues and ideologies.

4. Review the various agents of socialization, and note their respective contributions to the overall process of political socialization.

5. Describe the three rings of the mass media. Outline the mass media's three major functions. What is the importance to the media of structural bias and political bias?

6. What was the significance of the Stouffer research on tolerance in the 1950s? Have his predictions been borne out? Why or why not?

7. Discuss the influence of the electronic media on the conduct of government. Pay particular attention to the school of thought that views the electronic media as detrimental to governmental performance and the other school of thought that views it as making the government more powerful.

ANSWERS TO REVIEW QUESTIONS (WITH PAGE NUMBERS)

Multiple Choice

				Completion	
1.	a, p. 83	11.	c, p. 91	1.	legitimacy, p. 83
2.	b, p. 84	12.	d, p. 92	2.	Gallup, Harris, p. 85
3.	c, p. 84	13.	a, p. 90	3.	Chicago, p. 85
4.	d, p. 85	14.	c, p. 95	4.	65, p. 87
5.	d, p. 86	15.	a, p. 95	5.	liberal, p. 92
6.	d, p. 86-87	16.	d, p. 96	6.	group benefits, p. 89
7.	b, p. 87	17.	c, p. 97	7.	cognitive socialization, p. 95
8.	c, p. 88	18.	b, p. 98	8.	political party, p. 96
9.	b, p. 90	19.	b, p. 101	9.	television, p. 97
10.	d, p. 90	20.	c, p. 105	10.	agenda setting, p. 98

True-False

1.	F, p. 83	6.	T, p. 91
2.	T, p. 84	7.	T, p. 90
3.	T, p. 86	8.	T, p. 96
4.	T, p. 89	9.	F, p. 98
5.	F, p. 90	10.	T, p. 99

BEYOND THE TEXT: How to Watch the TV Election News

The objective of this exercise is to help you gain some insight into the way in which television networks cover the news. The special reference here is to the 1988 presidential election, but you can easily modify the exercise to make it apply to a nonelection news program if you are taking the American Government course when there is no election. This exercise also seeks to get you to ask whether the nightly television news shows exemplify some of the principles discussed in Chapter 4.

1. Pick an evening when you are free to give your undivided attention to one of the network news shows. Use a watch to record precisely the minutes and seconds devoted to each of the categories indicated in part I of the data sheet below. Then answer the questions in part II of the data sheet.

2. Pick up that day's and the next day's New York Times to compare its coverage of the same events to TV's coverage.

3. Discuss with friends in the class, get the instructor to discuss in class, or at least think about the following questions:
a. Did TV cover the issues as thoroughly as the newspaper?
b. Were there any examples of TV picking up the news from the newspaper or vice versa?
c. What percent of the TV news show was devoted to election news? How did this compare to the newspaper?
d. Did the TV election news give you substantive information about the candidates' stands on issues and on their abilities and qualifications to handle the job? How did this compare to the newspaper?
e. Was the TV news or the newspaper news more vulnerable to the criticism cited in the text of portraying politics as "a fantasy world . . . [that gives people] . . . little, if any, grasp of political processes or power structures"?
f. Was TV news or the newspaper more vulnerable to the other criticism cited in the text of fostering negative, antipolitician, antiestablishment biases?
g. What did you learn about the need to balance TV's portrayal of information with information from other sources?

DATA SHEET FOR PRESIDENTIAL ELECTION NEWS COVERAGE

Date _____   Network Watched _____   Time _____

I. Distribution of News Time
      Indicate below the number of minutes the newscast spent on:

      1. The presidential election   _____
      2. Other national political events   _____
      3. Other national nonpolitical events   _____
      4. State or metropolitan political news   _____
      5. State or metropolitan nonpolitical news   _____
      6. International news   _____
      7. Sports   _____
      8. Advertising   _____
      9. Weather   _____
     10. Other   _____

II. Quality of Election Coverage

      A. Did the newscast's coverage concentrate on:

          1. Issues?   _____
          2. Campaign schedules?   _____
          3. Personality of the candidates?   _____
          4. Human interest (candidates' families)?   _____
          5. Other?   _____

B. Comment on the extent to which the coverage of this newscast did or did not
help educate you on the campaign.

Chapter 5

POLITICAL PARTIES IN
AMERICAN DEMOCRACY

CHAPTER OUTLINE

Write a one-sentence summary of the materials found under each of the headings and
subheadings in the text:

LEARNING OBJECTIVES

After reading Chapter 5 and doing the exercises in this study guide, you should be able to:

1. Explain the four basic types of elections and the significance of the two-tiered party system.
2. Outline both the similarities and differences between the two major political parties.
3. Describe the organizational structure of the national political party, along with its key personnel and functions.
4. Analyze why party loyalties have been declining and the implications of that decline for the American political system.
5. Describe the impact party reform has had on the Democratic and Republican parties.
6. Explain the influence of the electronic media on political parties.

IDENTIFICATION ITEMS

Write out a one- or two-sentence identification that gives the significance of the following terms or names to this chapter:

Political party
Social issues
Realigning election
Deviating election
New Deal coalition
Ideological party
Tripartite party organization
National convention
Congressional campaign committee
Party platform
Party identification
Direct primary election
Latent function of machines
1968 Democratic convention
DO Committee
Proportional representation
Party as church
Party as coalition
Responsible party model
David Broder
Norman Thomas

George Wallace
Critical election period
Economic issues
Maintaining election
Reinstating election
Two-tiered system
Protest party
National committee
National chairperson
Ticket splitting
Political party machine
Manifest function of machines
McGovern-Fraser Commission
Unit rule
Amateur activist
New elite establishment
Multiparty system
Kevin Phillips
Robert LaFollette
John C. Anderson
Walter Dean Burnham

REVIEW QUESTIONS

Multiple Choice Questions

1. The most likely origin of today's Democratic party can be traced to:
    a. Thomas Jefferson
    b. Andrew Jackson
    c. Abraham Lincoln
    d. Alexander Hamilton

2. The Republican party became a major party in the period starting with:
   a. the Civil War   c. FDR's election
   b. the 1896 election   d. World War II

3. Which of the following issues has directly contributed to a period of
   Democratic party decay?
   a. depression   c. social issues
   b. unemployment   d. World War II

4. The election of 1932 was an example of what kind of election?
   a. deviating   c. reinstating
   b. maintaining   d. realigning

5. The elections of 1952 and 1956 exemplify what kind of elections?
   a. deviating   c. reinstating
   b. maintaining   d. realigning

6. The book The Emerging Republican Majority predicted that a new Republican era
   would start in the year:
   a. 1980   c. 1968
   b. 1972   d. 1964

7. The new class Democrats are:
   a. liberal on many important social issues
   b. blue-collar, non-college-educated voters
   c. both a and b
   d. conservative on most important social issues

8. Which of the following is probably not a core group of the Republican party?
   a. white Protestants   c. Catholics
   b. high-status jobholders   d. Westerners

9. According to voting records of Republican and Democratic senators:
   a. Democratic senators are more liberal than Republican ones
   b. Southern Democrats are more conservative than Republican senators
   c. Republican senators are more liberal than Democratic ones
   d. Southern Republicans are more liberal than northern Republicans

10. The third-party candidate who attracted 13 million popular votes and forty-six
    electoral votes was:
    a. Strom Thurmond   c. Robert LaFollette
    b. John C. Anderson   d. George Wallace

11. Which of the following is a task of the national convention?
    a. write a party platform
    b. promote party unity
    c. nominate the party's candidate for president
    d. all of the above

12. Both Bill Brock and Ray Bliss:
    a. have been presidential nominees
    b. have been successful national chairpersons
    c. have been governors of Democratic states
    d. were the joint authors of The Emerging Republican Majority

13. Which of the following is true?
    a. the percentage of pure independent voters has more than doubled since 1952
    b. the percentage of strong Democrats and Republicans has declined since 1952
    c. both a and b
    d. none of the above

14. By the mid-1970s, the percentage of ticket splitters had increased to about:
    a. 55 percent   c. 75 percent
    b. 25 percent   d. 10 percent

15. The McGovern-Fraser Commission:
    a. abolished the unit rule in the Democratic national convention
    b. sought proportional representation for women and minorities in the Democratic national convention
    c. both a and b
    d. none of the above; McGovern and Fraser were Republicans

16. In order for the Republicans to become the majority party, they need to win more converts from:
    a. black voters
    b. white ethnic voters
    c. Catholic voters
    d. all of the above

17. According to the text, the following statement is true regarding political parties and the future:
    a. the quality of American life is undermined by the decline of political parties
    b. the decline of parties threatens the least powerful class of people in American society
    c. both a and b
    d. none of the above

18. The text argues that parties can be strengthened by:
    a. increasing the power of the national committees
    b. public financing being given directly to the candidates
    c. reserving half of the convention delegate seats for elected public officials
    d. a and c, but not b

19. The new elite establishment refers to:
    a. strong Democratic voters
    b. blue-collar Democrats who might vote for the GOP
    c. independent voters
    d. none of these

20. Democratic national conventions in the 1970s were heavily influenced by:
    a. amateur activists   c. elected officeholders
    b. professional politicians   d. none of the above

Completion Questions

1. The first elected Republican president was _____.

2. Basic institutions for the translation of mass preferences into public policy
   are _____ _____.

3. The time period from 1860 to 1932 was dominated by the _____ party.

4. In 1968, third-party candidate _____ _____ proclaimed that
   there "isn't a dime's worth of difference between" the Democrat and Republican
   parties.

5. The Libertarian party, American Nazi party, and Socialist Workers party are
   examples of _____ third parties.

6. The description of the political parties as tripartite structures includes the
   party in _____, the party _____, and the party
   in _____.

7. The most dominant characteristic of American political parties is that they
   are _____.

8. Electing people to office and taking command of government are a political
   party's _____ functions, according to Robert Merton.

9. The three phases of party organizations since midcentury include the party as
   nominator, _____ and _____.

10. The central argument in favor of _____ systems is that they do a
    better job of representing a wider variety of people.

True-False Questions

T   F   1. Journalist David Broder argues that the decline of political parties
            may strengthen American democracy, not weaken it.

T   F   2. The New Deal coalition has entered into a period of decay.

T   F   3. Americans have a strong bias in favor of a multiparty political system.

T   F   4. Old Class Democrats tend to be liberal on both economic and social
            issues.

T   F   5. Party activists tend to be more ideological than regular party voters.

T F 6. Despite popular belief, party platforms are taken seriously by elected
         officials.

T F 7. Republican congressional campaign committees have been less successful
         than their Democratic counterparts.

T F 8. The newest, youngest voters are most likely to be Independents.

T F 9. Party reforms have increased the representation of minorities and women
         in the party conventions.

T F 10. The Democratic party is split between its economic and social policy
         liberals.

Mastery Questions

Outline a response to each of the following:

 1. How have America's political parties influenced America's economic and social
    development?

 2. Review and discuss Burnham's five stages of party alignment.

 3. Has a new realignment period of party politics occurred since 1932? Cite
    reasons for your answer.

 4. Explain two-tier voting and its significance for contemporary political
    parties.

 5. Cite some of the major differences between the Democratic and Republican
    parties.

 6. What is the basic role or function of protest parties? Cite some recent
    examples.

 7. Review the perils of the third-party candidate in 1980, Congressman John C.
    Anderson.

 8. In what ways have Congressional campaign committees become increasingly
    important?

 9. Discuss the impact of the electronic communications media on political parties.

10. Describe some of the party challenges and opportunities facing the Democrats
    and Republicans in the future.

ANSWERS TO REVIEW QUESTIONS (WITH PAGE NUMBERS)

Multiple Choice

1. b, p. 115	11. d, p. 133
2. a, p. 115	12. b, p. 133
3. c, p. 118	13. c, p. 135
4. d, p. 118	14. b, p. 137
5. a, p. 119	15. c, p. 136
6. c, p. 119	16. d, p. 139
7. a, p. 121	17. c, p. 141
8. c, p. 123	18. d, p. 142
9. a, p. 125	19. d, p. 139
10. d, p. 130	20. a, p. 138

Completion

1. Abraham Lincoln, p. 115
2. political parties, p. 116
3. Republican party, p. 117
4. George Wallace, p. 122
5. ideological, p. 128
6. electorate; organization; government, p. 130
7. decentralized, p. 131
8. manifest, p. 137
9. evaluator; shell, p. 138
10. multiparty, p. 127

True-False

1. F, p. 116	6. T, p. 133
2. T, p. 118	7. F, p. 134
3. F, p. 126	8. T, p. 135
4. F, p. 121	9. T, p. 138
5. T, p. 124	10. T, p. 140

BEYOND THE TEXT: Parties in Congress: How Strong?

How deep is party strength in Congress? And how closely is the party line followed by your representative and senators? You can gain valuable insight into these questions by examining one of the most useful reference works on Congress, The Congressional Quarterly (or CQ). CQ publishes a weekly report and an end-of-the-year Congressional Quarterly Almanac. Examine the voting studies section (usually Appendix C) of the most recent CQ Almanac, and use the information there to answer the following questions:

1. Comparing the most recent year's party unity score with those for prior years, is the trend toward greater or lesser party unity?

2. Which party grouping has the highest and lowest party unity? Senate Democrats? Senate Republicans? House Democrats? House Republicans?

3. Which party grouping has the highest and lowest sectional unity? Which sectional grouping?

4. How does the CQ measure party unity and sectional unity?

5. Which party grouping provides the greatest presidential support? Senate Democrats? Senate Republicans? House Democrats? House Republicans?

6. How strong is the conservative coalition? On which issues did it surface the most? Which individual senators and representatives provided the most support for the conservative coalition? the most opposition?

7. Examining the data for your representative and senators, what are their scores on: party unity? sectional unity? presidential support? conservative coalition?

8. To what extent are the voting patterns which you have just observed consistent with the voting patterns discussed in the text, especially in reference to: presidential support (see Chapter 9)? the conservative coalition (see Chapter 8)? party unity?

Chapter 6

ELECTIONS IN AMERICAN DEMOCRACY

CHAPTER OUTLINE

Write a one-sentence summary of the materials found under each of the headings and subheadings in the text:

LEARNING OBJECTIVES

After reading Chapter 6 and doing the exercises in this study guide, you should be able to:

1. Describe thoroughly the presidential election process, noting the three phases of early maneuvering, the battle for nomination, and the general election campaign.
2. Explain the workings of the electoral college, along with its relative strengths, weaknesses, and proposed reforms.
3. Outline the campaign finance laws and why problems persist in this area.
4. Summarize those factors which persuade people to vote or not to vote, including socioeconomic status, long-term forces, and short-term forces.
5. Explain why elections do not provide mandates.
6. List the important functions of elections within a democratic political system.

IDENTIFICATION ITEMS

Write out a one- or two-sentence identification that gives the significance of the following terms or names to this chapter:

Early maneuvering
Nominating caucus
New Hampshire primary
Democratic coalition
Democratic strategic problem
Reagan 1984 strategy
Gender gap
Televised debate
Electoral college reform plans
Gerrymandering
Coattail phenomenon
1925 Corrupt Practices Act
Buckley v. Valeo
Gladiator
Nonparticipant
Nonvoters (6 types of)
Retrospective judgment
Poll tax
Grandfather clause

Horse-race campaign coverage
Great Mentionizer
Direct presidential primary
Iowa caucuses
Republican coalition
Republican strategic problem
Mondale 1984 strategy
Daisy girl commercial
Electoral college
Midterm (off-year) election
Surge and decline theory
Federal Elections Campaign Act
Political action committee
Spectator
Voter registration requirements
Voting Rights Act of 1965
Literacy test
White primary
Faithless elector

REVIEW QUESTIONS

Multiple Choice Questions

1. In the 1984 presidential election, the Republicans:
   a. won the presidency
   b. kept control of the Senate
   c. kept control of the House
   d. both a and b

2. Which one of the following politicians was not engaged in early maneuvering
   for the 1988 Republican presidential nomination?
   a. Howard Baker   c. Jack Kemp
   b. George Bush   d. Gary Hart

3. Two key early presidential candidate tests are in the states of:
   a. New Hampshire and Iowa   c. California and Florida
   b. New York and Virginia   d. Texas and Illinois

4. Increasing the voter turnout of racial minorities and low-income voters is
   usually considered a strategic consideration favoring the:
   a. Republicans
   b. Democrats
   c. Neither a nor b, because it would favor both major parties
   d. Libertarian party

5. Most voters usually make up their minds on the presidential candidate they
   will vote for:
   a. a year before the election
   b. by the end of the convention
   c. after the first television debate
   d. the day before the election

6. Making a nonpartisan appeal to union member voters in hopes of switching them
   from their traditional voting allegiances is usually considered a strategic
   aim of:
   a. nobody; union members' loyalties are so deeply entrenched that they are
      seldom changeable
   b. racial minority candidates seeking the Republican party presidential
      nomination
   c. the Democratic nominee for president
   d. the Republican nominee for president

7. PINS is:
   a. an important PAC for the GOP
   b. a new code for financing campaigns
   c. a computerized polling system used by President Reagan
   d. an opinion-tracking system used by President Carter

8. The classic daisy girl political commercial was directed at:
   a. Lyndon Johnson   c. Ronald Reagan
   b. Edward Kennedy   d. Barry Goldwater

9. The section of the country most solidly Republican in presidential elections since 1952 has been the:
   a. South
   b. Northeast
   c. West
   d. Midwest

10. Concerning the gender gap, public opinion polling and the election results of 1984 suggest that:
    a. there really is no gender gap
    b. there is a gender gap, but it is unclear which parties or candidates are most favored by it
    c. there is a gender gap, and it favors the Democrats
    d. there is a gender gap, and it favors the Republicans

11. Defenders of the electoral college argue that it:
    a. stabilizes the two-party system
    b. promotes the interests of the small states
    c. helps the interests of minorities
    d. all of the above

12. Under the proposed proportional plan reform of the electoral college:
    a. John Kennedy would have been elected president in 1960
    b. Richard Nixon would have been elected president in 1960
    c. neither man would have been elected
    d. third-party candidate George Wallace would not have received any electoral votes in 1968

13. Which of the following is true?
    a. Senate races are usually more competitive than House races
    b. in only five midterm elections since 1934 has the president's party gained seats in Congress
    c. voter turnout rates in midterm elections usually exceed those of congressional elections during the presidential election years
    d. the president's party usually wins seats in Congress in the midterm elections

14. The major complaint against horse-race coverage of election campaigns is that:
    a. such coverage spends too much time on issues and fails to inform voters about who is leading in the contest
    b. such coverage tends to trivialize elections
    c. such coverage tends to be biased in favor of the Democrats
    d. such coverage tends to be biased in favor of the Republicans

15. Buckley v. Valeo:
    a. gave an advantage to wealthy candidates
    b. actually strengthened the influence of national parties in elections
    c. struck down the system of publicly funded presidential elections
    d. overturned the Voting Rights Act of 1965

16. Public funding of congressional elections:
    a. was provided by the 1974 campaign finance law
    b. has largely eliminated the influence of PACs
    c. has successfully democratized congressional elections
    d. was not passed into law

17. According to Lester Milbrath, the majority of Americans whose political involvement is limited to voting regularly are termed:
    a. gladiators
    b. spectators
    c. positive apathetics
    d. nay sayers

18. If voter registration requirements were relaxed to the level of the least restrictive state, Rosenstone and Wolfinger estimate that voter turnout would increase by:
    a. 51 percent
    b. 22 percent
    c. 9 percent
    d. none of the above; there is no way to make such estimates

19. In the years following the Voting Rights Act of 1965, there was a dramatic increase in the number of black officeholders and a decline in blatantly racist election campaigns. These facts were cited by the text as evidence that:
    a. elections give mandates
    b. elections can help protect people from abuses
    c. elections are principally exercises in retrospective judgments by voters
    d. elections do not give mandates

20. In the viewpoint section, the text suggests improving the U.S. election system by:
    a. direct popular election of the president
    b. allowing PACs more financial autonomy
    c. both a and b
    d. neither a nor b

Completion Questions

1. The Democratic vice-presidential nominee in 1984 was _____.

2. A state's delegates to the national convention are chosen by the caucus/convention method or by a _____ _____.

3. An electoral college elector who refuses to cast his/her vote as the state's popular vote determined is referred to as a/an _____ _____.

4. The Democratic party's three largest voter groups are _____, _____, and _____.

5. There are a total of _____ electoral votes in the electoral college.

6. The national bonus plan would award _____ bonus votes to the winner of the national popular vote.

7. The surge and decline theory, or _____ phenomenon, is one explanation of the loss of House seats by the president's party in midterm elections.

8. PAC stands for _____ _____ _____.

9. The most important variable influencing voter turnout is _____.

10. Issues and candidate attractiveness represent _____ term influences on voting behavior.

True-False Questions

T   F   1. In House of Representative campaigns for reelection, 90 to 95 percent of incumbents seeking reelection usually win.

T   F   2. The caucus-convention method gives voters a direct voice in selecting national convention delegates.

T   F   3. A voting group's size, regularity of voting turnout, and loyalty to party nominees all determine its impact upon the popular vote.

T   F   4. There is more substantive information contained in TV commercials for candidates than is found in network news shows.

T   F   5. In recent years, Democrats have gotten a much smaller share of seats in the House of Representatives than would be warranted by their percentage of the vote in congressional races, but Republicans have gotten a much smaller percent of Senate seats than would be warranted by their percentage of the vote.

T   F   6. In 1984 the Supreme Court prohibited PACs such as the National Conservative Political Action Committee from making independent expenditures on behalf of President Reagan's reelection campaign.

T   F   7. In comparing the variables of income, educational level, and attachment to organizations, it was found that income had the biggest impact on voter turnout.

T   F   8. Under the Federal Elections Campaign Act, individuals are limited to contributing no more than $1,000 per election to any one federal candidate.

T   F   9. In studying the gender gap, survey researchers have found almost no difference between the opinions of men and women on foreign policy and domestic welfare issues.

T   F   10. The poll tax, white primary, and literacy tests were all outlawed by the Twenty-fourth Amendment.

Mastery Questions

Outline a response to each of the following:

1. What are the four tasks involved for a presidential candidate in the early maneuvering phase?

2. Review the key events of both Reagan's and Mondale's nomination and general election battles in 1984.

3. What are the three strategic problems regarding popular vote strategy for the Democratic presidential nominees? What are the strategic problems for Republican nominees?

4. Summarize the debate over the electoral college and evaluate the various proposed reforms suggested to change the current electoral framework.

5. Why do congressional incumbents enjoy such a major reelection advantage over their challengers?

6. Why was the 1925 Corrupt Practices ineffective? How did the Federal Elections Campaign Act of 1974 attempt to achieve election finance reform?

7. Discuss the merits and demerits of the role that PACs play in the election process.

8. Review the fundamental reasons why the rate of political participation has been declining in the country. List and briefly describe the six different types of nonvoters.

9. In what sense does an election represent a retrospective judgement by voters?

ANSWERS TO REVIEW QUESTIONS (WITH PAGE NUMBERS)

Multiple Choice

1.	d, p. 150	11.	d, p. 165
2.	d, p. 151	12.	c, p. 165
3.	a, p. 152	13.	a, p. 168
4.	b, p. 156	14.	b, p. 160
5.	b, p. 154	15.	a, p. 171
6.	d, p. 155	16.	d, p. 173
7.	c, p. 158	17.	b, p. 173
8.	d, p. 159	18.	c, p. 174
9.	c, p. 163	19.	b, p. 182
10.	b, p. 158	20.	a, p. 183

Completion

1. Geraldine Ferraro, p. 157
2. primary election, p. 152
3. faithless elector, p. 165
4. union members, Catholic, South, p. 154
5. 538, p. 164
6. 102, p. 167
7. coattail, p. 168
8. political action committee, p. 171
9. education, p. 174
10. short, p. 10

True-False

1.	T, p. 167	6.	F, p. 171
2.	F, p. 152	7.	F, p. 175
3.	T, p. 154	8.	T, p. 170
4.	T, p. 159	9.	F, p. 157
5.	F, p. 168	10.	F, p. 178

BEYOND THE TEXT: How to Watch the Media Watch an Election

In the Chapter 3 section, we set up some criteria for evaluating television news broadcast coverage of an election. In this chapter we examine some other aspects of TV election coverage. Although the focus here is on the 1988 presidential election, the activities can easily be modified to relate to races in your state or locality. There are three different activities to this exercise:

1. If there is a televised debate, watch the debate. If you are observing a local election which has no televised debate, attend a debate between the candidates.

2. Describe and criticize five different televised political commercials. Try to pick commercials from different candidates and different elections. How long does the commercial last? Does it deal with personalities, issues, or what? Does it appeal to reason or to emotions? Does it promote simplistic answers to complex problems? If this commercial were a person's only source of information about the election, would that person be able to make an intelligent choice?

3. Review your comments on television network newscasts made in the Chapter 3 Beyond the Text section.

Having gathered this information on newscasts, debates, and commercials, discuss with your friends or in class how each mode of television coverage helped you as an individual understand: the capabilities of the presidential candidates; the issues of the campaign; the underlying problems that government must confront; the limitations on our government in dealing with these problems. Which mode did you find the most useful? the least?

Chapter 7

POLITICAL INTEREST GROUPS

CHAPTER OUTLINE

Write a one-sentence summary of the materials found under each of the headings and subheadings in the text:

LEARNING OBJECTIVES

After reading Chapter 7 and doing the exercises in this study guide, you should be able to:

1. Explain the contributions and roles of interest groups within a democratic political system.
2. Itemize the main categories of interest groups, noting prominent specific groups by name within each category.
3. Summarize the four types of interest group tactics, including specific examples of each tactic in practice.
4. Explain the relationship of interest groups to public policy, with special attention to the topics of policy initiation, single-issue groups, and biases.
5. Distinguish between elitist and pluralist theories of American politics.
6. Compare and contrast the relative strengths and weaknesses of interest groups in the American political system.

IDENTIFICATION ITEMS

Write out a one- or two-sentence identification that gives the significance of the following terms or names to this chapter:

Political interest group
Material incentives
Purposive incentives
Potential interest group
Business Round Table
Teamsters
Taft-Hartley Act of 1947
Union shop
PATCO
Givebacks
PIRG
Women's movement
Single-issue group
Indirect lobbying
1946 Regulation of Lobbying Act
U.S. v. Harris
Defensive lobbying
Council on Foreign Relations
Iron Law of Oligarchy
Elitist theory
James Madison

Roberto Michels
Solidarity incentives
Lobbyists' Row
Types of interest groups
Chamber of Commerce
National Labor Relations Act
Collective bargaining
AFL-CIO
Free-rider problem
Civil Rights movement
Lobbying
Litigation
Political action committee
NCPAC
Robinson v. Cahill
Moral Majority
Policy Planning Institute
Pluralist theory
C. Wright Mills
David Truman
Richard Viguerie

REVIEW QUESTIONS

Multiple Choice Questions

1. According to James Madison, the public interest could be served by:
   a. eliminating factions
   b. allowing ambition to check ambition
   c. permitting interest groups to replace political parties
   d. permitting the expansion of factions

2. In David Truman's view, potential interest groups are converted into actual interest groups by:
   a. legal contracts
   b. Supreme Court rulings
   c. social upheaval
   d. congressional actions

3. The Business Roundtable is:
   a. composed solely of corporate chief executives
   b. a small policy-advisory group to the president
   c. now defunct, replaced by another business group
   d. a bipartisan, joint labor-business organization

4. Which of the following groups has the least to contend with in dealing with the free-rider problem?
   a. Common Cause
   b. PIRGs
   c. AFL-CIO
   d. Natural Gas Association

5. The number of workers who belong to unions is:
   a. 13 million; one-fifth of the labor force
   b. 33 million; one-third of the labor force
   c. 23 million; one-fourth of the labor force
   d. 13 million; one-tenth of the labor force

6. As an interest group tactic in the 1980s, litigation has been:
   a. on the decline
   b. avoided by conservative groups
   c. primarily a tool of liberal groups
   d. increasingly practiced by conservative groups

7. In the early 1980s, a major example of givebacks occurred between:
   a. PATCO and the federal government
   b. Chrysler and the UAW
   c. AFT and the NEA
   d. the Business Roundtable and the AFL-CIO

8. The professional interest group of lawyers is the:
   a. AMA
   b. ABA
   c. LIG
   d. AFT

9. Common Cause is an example of a:
   a. public-interest group
   b. business interest group
   c. labor interest group
   d. professional interest group

10. PIRGs:
    a. were originally set up by Ralph Nader
    b. are funded by university students
    c. have demonstrated a concern with environmental and consumer goals
    d. all of the above

11. Political movements:
    a. are usually represented by a single interest group
    b. usually seek significant social change
    c. both a and b
    d. neither a nor b

12. According to the text, congressional campaign contributions were highest from:
    a. health PACs   c. corporate PACs
    b. labor PACs   d. nonconnected PACs

13. Which theory would be most likely to argue that competition between interest groups leads to the public good, and which theory would probably argue that powerful private institutions effectively control the government?
    a. Pluralist; pluralist   c. Elitist; pluralist
    b. Pluralist; elitist   d. Elitist; elitist

14. In Robinson v. Cahill, the lawsuit was initiated by:
    a. Kenneth Robinson   c. a coalition of interest groups
    b. Edward Cahill   d. the State of New Jersey

15. Probably the most effective tactic used by lobbyists is:
    a. bribery   c. providing information
    b. wining and dining   d. threats

16. Studies show that lobbying:
    a. is consistently successful in its persuasive efforts
    b. has had significant impact upon congressional appropriations
    c. both a and b
    d. none of the above

17. The Reverend Jerry Falwell and his moral majority are associated with:
    a. indirect lobbying   c. interest-group litigation
    b. direct lobbying   d. bribery

18. Interest groups are biased:
    a. toward the status quo
    b. toward the middle and upper class
    c. both a and b
    d. toward the lower classes

19. According to Michels, oligarchic tendencies are:
    a. common mainly to large organizations
    b. common mainly to smaller organizations
    c. common to all groups
    d. common only to military bureaucracies

20. Which is not a suggestion made by the Viewpoint section of the text?
    a. tax credits for interest group membership among the poor
    b. increasing funding limits for PACs
    c. tougher regulation of lobbying activities
    d. strengthened political parties

Completion Questions

1. A group of people who organize to influence public policy is termed a political _____ _____.

2. The three major categories of economic interest groups are _____, _____, and _____.

3. The two dominant labor organizations are the _____ and the _____.

4. The AFT stands for the _____ _____ _____.

5. The National Association of County Officials is a/an _____ _____ group.

6. A committee created by an interest group for the purpose of raising funds to elect candidates favored by the group is termed a _____ _____ committee.

7. Ideological groups often find it easier to attract members and raise money in times of _____ than in _____ times.

8. According to David Truman, defensive lobbying is dedicated to protecting the _____ _____.

9. The NAACP is best associated with the interest-group activity of _____.

10. The Council on Foreign Relations and the American Enterprise Institute are termed _____ _____ institutes.

True-False Questions

T   F   1. Ideological satisfactions from seeing some public good accomplished refers to an interest group's purposive incentives.

T   F   2. Regarding business interest groups, large-sized groups exert the most influence on public policy.

T   F   3. The union shop is legal due to the Taft-Hartley Act and other labor legislation.

T   F   4. The oldest teachers' association is the NEA.

T   F   5. The Gallup Poll found that few Americans contribute to public interest groups.

T   F   6. PACs can contribute up to $10,000 each to congressional campaigns.

T   F   7. In the <u>United States</u> v. <u>Harris</u> the Supreme Court ruled that the Federal Regulation of Lobbying Act was unconstitutional.

T   F   8. Single-issue interest groups are usually ready to compromise on policy solutions.

T   F   9. The interest-group system is biased in favor of the lower classes.

T   F   10. Pluralist theory was made famous by C. Wright Mills.

Mastery Questions

Outline a response to each of the following:

1. Why, within a given category of interest groups, is there frequently more conflict than cooperation? Cite some specific examples.

2. What are likely to be some of the major challenges facing labor unions in the future?

3. What are the methods by which public-interest groups finance their activities?

4. What are some loopholes in the Federal Regulation of Lobbying Act?

5. Summarize the differences between pluralist and elitist theory.

6. Outline the strengths and weaknesses of the interest group system.

ANSWERS TO REVIEW QUESTIONS (WITH PAGE NUMBERS)

Multiple Choice   Completion

 1. b, p. 190   11. b, p. 198   1. interest group, p. 189
 2. c, p. 191   12. c, p. 201   2. business, labor, and farming,
 3. a, p. 192   13. b, p. 208   p. 192
 4. d, p. 198   14. c, p. 204   3. AFL-CIO, Teamsters, p. 193
 5. c, p. 193   15. c, p. 202   4. American Federation of
 6. d, p. 204   16. d, p. 203   Teachers, p. 195
 7. b, p. 194   17. a, p. 204   5. public agency, p. 198
 8. b, p. 195   18. c, p. 207   6. political action, p. 201
 9. a, p. 196   19. c, p. 207   7. adversity, good, p. 202
10. d, p. 197   20. b, p. 212   8. status quo, p. 203
                                          9. litigation, p. 204
                                         10. policy planning, p. 205

True-False

1. T, p. 192
2. F, p. 192
3. T, p. 194
4. T, p. 195
5. F, p. 197

6. F, p. 201
7. F, p. 207
8. F, p. 206
9. F, p. 207
10. F, p. 209

BEYOND THE TEXT: Evaluating Interest Groups in Your Life

Your daily life offers an opportunity to test some of the principles discussed in this chapter, since a number of interest groups may affect you personally. Does your campus have a student government organization? a PIRG? a College Democrat or College Republican club? some other campus organization that might concern you? Do you belong to a church? a labor union? some civic organization? any other group? Is there any organization in your neighborhood with meetings open to the public, such as a Democratic or Republican party club? a neighborhood association? a human relations council? a local government advisory board?

Choose one of these organizations and attend the next few meetings. Observe these meetings and comment on the extent to which the chapter's generalizations about group behavior apply or do not apply to the groups you observe in person.

1. Can the initial formation of your group be explained by the theories of interest-group creation discussed in the chapter? Explain.

2. Are the people attending the meetings attracted primarily by material incentives, solidarity incentives, or purposive incentives?

3. Into which category of groups does your group best fit?

4. Where does your group obtain the financing needed to function? Does it face a free-rider problem? If not, why not? If so, how does it cope with that problem?

5. Does your group belong to part of any social movement? If so, what is the connection?

6. If your group is affected in any way by government actions, what tactics does it use to bring its influence to bear upon the government? Does it use any of the tactics discussed in the chapter? Does it use any tactics not discussed? Elaborate.

7. How does your group stand on single-issue politics? Are its members uncompromising on any issues? Do they seek to influence public policy on that issue?

8. Does your group exhibit any of the tendencies of the Iron Law of Oligarchy? Who sets the agendas for the meetings? Who controls the meetings? Who recruits leaders for the group? How? How long have the current leaders been in office? What percent of the membership attends the meetings? Are there any important divergences between the interests of the members and those of the leaders?

9. Does your group exhibit any of the biases discussed in the text?

Chapter 8

CONGRESS AND THE POLITICS
OF LEGISLATING POLICY

CHAPTER OUTLINE

Write a one-sentence summary of the materials found under each of the headings and subheadings in the text:

LEARNING OBJECTIVES

After reading Chapter 8 and doing the exercises in this study guide, you should be able to:

1. Explain the various institutional obstacles which confront a bill before it becomes a law.
2. Identify the leadership positions of both houses of Congress and analyze their major functions.
3. Discuss the specific controversies over impoundment, war powers, executive privilege, and legislative veto, noting how these issues have contributed to the conflict between Congress and the president.
4. Understand the connection between democratization of Congress and the dispersal of influence.
5. Delineate the respective strengths and weaknesses of Congress as a political institution.
6. Describe the personal, professional, economic, and social backgrounds of members of Congress and the nature of their relationships with constituents.
7. Explain how television coverage of Congress has led to worsening the image of Congress as an institution, while improving the images of most individual members of Congress.

IDENTIFICATION ITEMS

Write out a one- or two-sentence identification that gives the significance of the following terms or names to this chapter:

Bill S790
Committee organization
Types of committees
Seniority rule
Sunshine rule
Party leadership positions
Party leadership organizations
Appropriations
Authorization
President pro tempore
Conservative coalition
Congressional support agencies
Casework
Legislative folkways
Cloture
Filibuster by amendment
Committee of the Whole
Veto
Show horse
War Powers Resolution of 1973
Constituent
Delegate role
Ombudsman
Package legislation

Henry Clay
Uncle Joe Cannon
Budget and Impoundment Control
   Act of 1974
Bicameralism
Party organization
Most prestigious committees
Subcommittee bill of rights
Legislative staff workers
Quorum
Discharge petition
Filibuster
Rider
Pocket veto
Veto override
Workhorse
Executive privilege
Trustee role
Politico role
Pork barrel
Social Security reform, 1983
Recission
Edmund Burke
Robert Dole

Deferral   James Wright
Legislative veto   Thomas B. (Czar) Reed
Pete V. Domenici   Lyndon B. Johnson
Tip O'Neill   Sam Rayburn

REVIEW QUESTIONS

Multiple Choice Questions

1. According to Madison, the chamber of Congress most susceptible to sudden and violent passions was:
   a. the House   c. both houses equally
   b. the Senate   d. neither

2. Which of the following standing committees is not usually thought of as a high-prestige committee?
   a. House Rules   c. Senate Finance
   b. House Ways and Means   d. House Ethics

3. The subcommittee bill of rights:
   a. strengthened the power of committee chairs
   b. allowed members to chair more than one subcommittee
   c. both a and b
   d. helped disperse influence in Congress

4. The person expected to succeed Tip O'Neill as Speaker of the House after O'Neill retires is:
   a. James Wright   c. Phil Gramm
   b. Howard Baker   d. Henry Clay

5. Party whips function primarily to:
   a. communicate grievances to the party leaders
   b. make sure that each bill's supporters vote on the floor
   c. decide which bills the party leadership should support
   d. determine committee assignments

6. The conservative coalition is a loose voting alliance of:
   a. Western Democrats and southern Republicans
   b. Southern Democrats and conservative Republicans
   c. conservatives within the eastern states
   d. Southern Republicans and northern Democrats

7. Which of the following is not a congressional support agency?
   a. Library of Congress
   b. Congressional Research Service
   c. Congressional Bureau of Investigation
   d. General Accounting Office

8. Discharge petitions:
   a. are very often successful
   b. require a majority vote of the House members
   c. are used most frequently in the Senate
   d. apply only to subcommittees

53

9. A cloture vote:
   a. requires at least sixty senatorial votes
   b. usually is difficult to pass
   c. is an attempt to end a filibuster
   d. all of the above

10. Congress can override a presidential veto by a:
    a. two-thirds vote of each house
    b. simple majority vote of each house
    c. two-thirds vote of the Senate, but a simple majority vote of the House of Representatives
    d. a simple majority vote of the House of Representatives, but a two-thirds vote of the Senate

11. A pocket veto occurs:
    a. when Congress fails to override a president's veto
    b. when the president signs a bill, then changes his mind and vetoes it by putting it in his pocket
    c. when there are less than 15 days left in the session of Congress and the president vetoes the bill after Congress overrides it
    d. when there are less than 10 days left in the session of Congress and the president does not sign a bill passed by Congress

12. Unlike Senator Domenici, Senator Russell Long favored:
    a. a user's tax for S790
    b. a fuel tax for S790
    c. an income tax for S790
    d. a property tax for S790

13. The rule of reciprocity often leads to a situation of "I'll vote for your bill if you vote for mine," or:
    a. accommodation   c. logrolling
    b. institutional loyalty   d. showboating

14. Under the Budget and Impoundment Control Act of 1974:
    a. a president can defer expenditures from one year to the next
    b. a president can make a decision to cancel expenditures if he notifies Congress in advance and Congress does not overrule his decision
    c. both a and b
    d. a president must spend immediately every cent that Congress appropriates

15. Which president attempted in 1973 to impound billions of dollars?
    a. Richard Nixon   c. Jimmy Carter
    b. Gerald Ford   d. Lyndon Johnson

16. The legislative veto:
    a. was upheld by the Supreme Court in 1983
    b. was struck down by the Supreme Court in 1983
    c. is still under consideration by the Supreme Court
    d. is not scheduled to be reviewed by the Supreme Court until 1990

17. Under the War Powers Resolution, the president has a total of how many days to complete the withdrawal of American forces once he has committed them to action?
    a. 60
    b. 30
    c. 90
    d. 120

18. The most underrepresented category of people among the members of Congress is:
    a. women
    b. blacks
    c. white professionals
    d. the poor

19. Package legislation was more prominent in legislation dealing with:
    a. ABSCAM
    b. Social Security
    c. energy
    d. War Powers Resolution

20. The text suggests which of the following proposals for improving Congress?
    a. strengthening the national parties
    b. making Congress less vulnerable to factions
    c. exercising restraint
    d. all of the above

Completion Questions

1. A two-house legislature is called a _____ legislature.

2. _____ committees are composed of senators and representatives who reach compromises on bills that passed the House in a different version than the Senate.

3. Sam Rayburn, Henry Clay, and Thomas Reed all held which Congressional post? _____ ___ ___ _____.

4. The current Senate Majority Leader is _____ _____.

5. Most bills in Congress die in _____.

6. Extraneous provisions tacked onto a bill to please groups of constituents or campaign contributors are termed _____.

7. The presidential process (outlawed in 1973) in which presidents refused to spend money appropriated by Congress is termed _____.

8. The _____ War (1950-1953) and the _____ War (1965-1973) were actions carried out without a formal declaration of war.

9. According to Burke, _____ are those who believe that their role is to vote according to the dictates of conscience.

10. Lock and Dam 26 was a good example of _____ _____ legislation, since it brought many jobs into an Illinois congressional district.

True-False Questions

T F 1. Individual representatives serve on more committees than do individual senators.

T F 2. Committee chairs are usually selected according to the seniority rule.

T F 3. The dispersion of influence is much greater in the House than in the Senate.

T F 4. The General Accounting Office (GAO) makes sure that congressional staffs are adequately staffed.

T F 5. Congressional staff workers do not play a major role in policymaking.

T F 6. The House of Representatives has a strong tradition of filibuster.

T F 7. Conference committee reports cannot be amended on the floor of the House or the Senate.

T F 8. Domenici's strategy of bypassing House consideration of his original bill brought into play the legislative folkway of institutional loyalty.

T F 9. The most popular role for most members of Congress is that of politico.

T F 10. Television coverage of Congress as a whole tends to be more negative than positive.

Mastery Questions

Outline a response to each of the following:

1. Why does Congress move like a glacier? Make your answer complete. Use the example of S790 in your reply. Make sure you list some of the possible hurdles and obstacles a bill must go through before passing into law.

2. Review the powers and duties of the Speaker of the House and the Majority Leader of the Senate. Cite a successful example of each and indicate what made them so effective.

3. Cite some reasons for the weak party discipline in Congress. In what way is this illustrated by Senator Phil Gramm?

4. Give a complete description of the War Powers Resolution of 1973.

5. Summarize suggested procedures to reform congressional practices and improve congressional ethics. Why does the text use the term "unintended consequences" in reference to the results of previous reforms? Would the suggested reforms avoid these unintended consequences if enacted? Why or why not?

6. Outline how Congress reacted to the shaping of energy policy in the 1970s and the need for Social Security reform in 1983. What strengths and weaknesses of Congress are exhibited by its handling of energy policy and Social Security reform?

ANSWERS TO REVIEW QUESTIONS (WITH PAGE NUMBERS)

Multiple Choice   Completion

1. a, p. 222   11. d, p. 235   1. bicameralism, p. 222
2. d, p. 224   12. b, p. 235   2. conference, p. 225
3. d, p. 225   13. c, p. 237   3. Speaker of the House, p. 228
4. a, p. 227   14. c, p. 238   4. Dole (1986), Byrd (1987), p. 227
5. b, p. 229   15. a, p. 237   5. committee, p. 233
6. b, p. 229   16. b, p. 238   6. riders, p. 235
7. c, p. 232   17. c, p. 238   7. impoundment, p. 237
8. b, p. 233   18. d, p. 240   8. Korean, Vietnam, p. 238
9. d, p. 233   19. b, p. 242   9. trustees, p. 240
10. a, p. 235   20. d, p. 249   10. pork-barrel, p. 241

True-False

1. F, p. 224   6. F, p. 233
2. T, p. 225   7. T, p. 235
3. F, p. 223   8. T, p. 237
4. F, p. 232   9. T, p. 241
5. F, p. 232   10. T, p. 247

BEYOND THE TEXT: Getting to Know Your Representative in Congress

How well do you know your representative in Congress? And the district in which you live? Is he or she liberal? conservative? Republican or Democratic? a leader or follower? To what extent does he or she mirror the constituency in which you live? The answers to these and similar questions can be found in two very useful reference books in your library or the nearest large university library: The Almanac of American Politics and the Congressional District Data Book. This exercise will familiarize you with these valuable resources, help you to know your representative better, and shed some light on the district in which you live. Use these resources to find the following information:

On the District

Median age   Median family income
Percent high school graduates   Percent in poverty
Occupational distribution   Percent of families with female head
Ethnic composition   Unemployment rate
Percent urban

On the Representative

Age
Education
Profession
Ethnic background
Religion
Salary
Political party
Years in Congress
Committee assignment
Committee leadership position
Party leadership position

Special interest caucuses in Congress
Prior occupational or political
    experience
Margins of victory in previous elections
Political Party
Political ideology as measured by:
    COPE index
    ACA index
    ADA index
Sources of political financial support

Chapter 9

THE PRESIDENCY AND THE
QUEST FOR LEADERSHIP

CHAPTER OUTLINE

Write a one-sentence summary of the materials found under each of the headings and
subheadings in the text:

LEARNING OBJECTIVES

After reading Chapter 9 and doing the exercises in this study guide, you should be able to:

1. Specify the roles, powers, and limitations of the modern presidency.
2. Discuss the paradox of the presidency.
3. Explain the basic factors underlying presidential effectiveness and the means by which presidents exercise leadership.
4. Describe the components of the institutional presidency, with particular emphasis on the cabinet, White House Staff, OMB, NSC, and CEA.
5. Discuss the impact of the media on the conduct of the presidency.
6. Summarize both the dangers and opportunities facing the presidency and the American future.

IDENTIFICATION ITEMS

Write out a one- or two-sentence identification that gives the significance of the following terms or names to this chapter:

Presidential roles   Theodore Roosevelt
Presidential failures   Great presidents
Stewardship theory   Literalist theory
Presidential character   Institutional presidency
Active-positive president   Active-negative president
Cabinet   White House Office
Executive Office of the President   National Security Council
Office of Management and Budget   Impoundment
Vice presidency   Groupthink
National Security Adviser   Council of Economic Advisers
Executive privilege   Paradox of the presidency
Imperial presidency   Conservative coalition
Two presidencies thesis   Executive agreement
Power to persuade   Law of anticipated reactions
Wolfpack journalism   Impeachment
Watergate   Six-year term proposal
President as prime minister plan   New Deal
Textbook presidency   Abraham Lincoln
James Buchanan   William Howard Taft
James David Barber

REVIEW QUESTIONS

Multiple Choice Questions

1. President James Buchanan was a supporter of:
   a. the abolitionists
   b. a constitutional amendment to outlaw slavery
   c. state secession
   d. compromising with slaveholders in order to preserve the Union

2. The current salary of the president is:
   a. $150,000, plus $50,000 for expenses
   b. $250,000, plus $100,000 for expenses
   c. $200,000, plus $50,000 for expenses
   d. $100,000, plus $25,000 for expenses

3. Appointing department heads and seeing that laws are faithfully executed are duties associated with the presidential role of:
   a. chief executive
   b. chief diplomat
   c. chief of state
   d. commander-in-chief

4. Which of the following is a limitation on the president?
   a. the courts
   b. the bureaucracy
   c. public opinion
   d. all of the above

5. According to the text, which of the following presidents was ranked as a failure?
   a. Abraham Lincoln
   b. Warren Harding
   c. James K. Polk
   d. Woodrow Wilson

6. The Great Depression and World War II are crises associated with the presidency of:
   a. Franklin D. Roosevelt
   b. John F. Kennedy
   c. Harry S Truman
   d. Dwight D. Eisenhower

7. Which of the following presidents was a passive-positive?
   a. Franklin D. Roosevelt
   b. Woodrow Wilson
   c. Lyndon Johnson
   d. Ronald Reagan

8. Which of the following characteristics is typical of the active-negative president?
   a. rigidity
   b. secretiveness
   c. both a and b
   d. an open administration

9. Which is true about cabinet members?
   a. they have divided loyalties
   b. they usually make a lasting impact upon the bureaucracy
   c. they inevitably become close advisers of the president
   d. all of the above

10. The media as a limitation on the presidential effectiveness is exemplified most by the phenomenon of:
    a. horse-race journalism
    b. dog-track journalism
    c. sycophantic journalism
    d. wolfpack journalism

11. The executive office of the president was established by:
    a. Herbert Hoover in 1930
    b. Harry Truman in 1949
    c. Franklin Roosevelt in 1939
    d. Woodrow Wilson in 1920

12. Which of the following is a function of the White House staff?
    a. congressional liaison
    b. public policy coordination
    c. both a and b
    d. choosing the Speaker of the House

13. Which of the following is not true about the functions and duties of the Office of Management and Budget?
    a. it checks agency budget requests before they are sent to Congress
    b. it controls the release of funds to agencies
    c. it has extensive impoundment powers today
    d. it has extensive managerial powers

14. Which of the following is not a member of the National Security Council?
    a. the vice president
    b. the secretary of the Treasury
    c. the CIA director
    d. the chair of the Joint Chiefs of Staff

15. A congressional grouping that frustrated some Democratic presidents but worked to the advantage of President Reagan is the:
    a. conference committee   c. liberal coalition
    b. majority leader   d. conservative coalition

16. An executive agreement is:
    a. identical to a treaty
    b. unlike a treaty in that it does not require ratification by the Senate
    c. used far less frequently by presidents than formal treaties
    d. identical to executive privilege

17. The law of anticipated reactions is probably most relevant for members of:
    a. courts   c. Congress
    b. the bureaucracy   d. all of the above

18. The Watergate tapes revealed that:
    a. President Nixon had prior knowledge of the Watergate break-in
    b. President Nixon had been involved in an illegal coverup from the beginning
    c. President Nixon was innocent of involvement in the Watergate affair
    d. a and b, but not c

19. Which of the following statements is true?
    a. Presidential popularity usually soars after displays of military force.
    b. Presidential rhetoric has inflated expectations of presidential performance.
    c. Presidential isolation is likely to be a recurring problem.
    d. All of the above.

20. Which is a criticism of the proposal for a six-year presidential term of office?
    a. A president cannot be placed above politics.
    b. A president would be a lame duck from the start of his term of office.
    c. Both a and b.
    d. It would force the president to worry too much about reelection.

Completion Questions

1. "I am the last President of the United States" is a statement attributed to President _____ _____ .

2. Two constitutional qualifications to be president are that a person must be a _____ _____ citizen and at least _____ years old.

3. According to scholars of the presidency, the five greatest presidents were: _____, _____, _____, _____, and _____ .

4. According to James David Barber, the _____ _____ dimension taps how much energy a president spends at the job.

5. The _____ _____ includes presidential advisers, the executive office of the president, and the cabinet.

6. The _____ cabinet is more prestigious than the _____ cabinet.

7. The OMB stands for _____ _____ _____ _____ _____ .

8. NSC adviser Zbigniew Brzezinski served under President _____ .

9. According to presidential scholar Richard Neustadt, the essential power of the president is the power to _____ .

10. Reporters who continuously report in a negative way about the president and government are said to engage in _____ journalism.

True-False Questions

T   F   1. Lincoln carefully consulted with Congress before taking the necessary steps to conduct the war effort against the Confederacy.

T   F   2. The textbook vision of the presidency fails to recognize the real limitations upon presidential power.

T   F   3. The stewardship theory is associated with President Theodore Roosevelt.

T . F   4. President Lyndon Johnson's handling of the Vietnam War had little public support even when the war began.

T   F   5. According to James David Barber, passive-positive presidents are the most effective in office.

T   F   6. Over time, the cabinet has become a major advisory body for the president.

T F 7. In general, the influence of the White House staff has declined since the era of FDR.

T F 8. Vietnam and Watergate probably put an end for a while to the imperial presidency.

T F 9. From 1948 to 1975, the foreign policy initiatives of presidents were less likely to get through Congress than domestic policy initiatives.

T F 10. In 90 percent of the cases since World War II, the president's party has controlled both houses of Congress.

Mastery Questions

Outline a response to each of the following:

1. List and briefly explain the main constitutional powers and extraconstitutional roles of the president. Relate these powers and roles to the following concepts: the paradox of the presidency; the textbook presidency; the two presidencies.

2. Support or attack this assertion: A president following a literalist philosophy today would be doomed to failure.

3. Describe and assess the two conflicting views of the influence of television on the presidency.

4. What are the merits and demerits of the decentralization-open model of the White House Staff as distinct from the centralized chain of the command-closed model?

5. Review the basic factors that influence presidential-congressional relations. Speculate on how Watergate affected those relationships.

6. Summarize and react to the proposals for a six-year presidential term of office and the president as a prime minister.

ANSWERS TO REVIEW QUESTIONS (WITH PAGE NUMBERS)

Multiple Choice

					Completion	
1.	d, p. 257	11.	c, p. 268		1.	James Buchanan, p. 258
2.	c, p. 259	12.	c, p. 270		2.	native-born; 35 years, p. 259
3.	a, p. 260	13.	c, p. 273		3.	Lincoln, Washington, Franklin, Roosevelt, Thomas Jefferson, Theodore Roosevelt, p. 264
4.	d, p. 261	14.	b, p. 274			
5.	b, p. 264	15.	d, p. 277			
6.	a, p. 265	16.	b, p. 277		4.	active-passive, p. 265
7.	d, p. 267	17.	c, p. 278		5.	institutional presidency, p. 268
8.	c, p. 265	18.	b, p. 287		6.	inner, outer, p. 268
9.	a, p. 268	19.	d, p. 288		7.	Office of Management and Budget, p. 272
10.	d, p. 282	20.	c, p. 289			
					8.	Carter, p. 274
					9.	persuade, p. 278
					10.	wolfpack, p. 282

True-False

1.	F, p. 258	6.	F, p. 268
2.	T, p. 261	7.	F, p. 272
3.	T, p. 263	8.	T, p. 276
4.	F, p. 265	9.	F, p. 277
5.	F, p. 265	10.	F, p. 276

BEYOND THE TEXT: Watching the Media Watch the President

This project should give you some interesting experiences in evaluating sources of information and evaluating a presidential administration. For the next month, follow the media sources indicated below and follow the instructions given:

1. Read your hometown daily newspaper and clip articles dealing with the president.

2. Read the appropriate section in one of the national news magazines each week, reading Time one week, Newsweek the next, and U.S. News the next. Take notes on any relevant information.

3. Regularly scan the major opinion magazines (such as The Nation, The New Republic, National Review). Read any relevant articles.

4. Watch each of the following programs on television at least once:
   a. A regular network newscast
   b. Washington Week in Review (Friday, PBS)
   c. McNeil-Lehrer News Hour (nightly, PBS)
   d. Nightline (nightly, ABC)
   e. McLaughlin Group (Sundays, PBS)

5. Regularly read the columns of one of the columnists in each of the following categories. Clip the most relevant columns.

Category 1	Category 2	Category 3
Jeanne Kirkpatrick	Tom Wicker	David Broder
Cal Thomas	Colman McCarthy	Tom Braden
George Will	Edwin Yoder	Anthony Lewis
William Safire	Richard Cohen	James Reston

As you use these sources of information, keep asking the following questions:

1. Does this source reflect left or right ideologies?

2. Is the appeal to emotion or to reason?

3. Does the source present more than one side of an issue before making a judgment?

4. Does the source support viewpoints with accurate facts?

5. Does the source twist facts to support the argument?

6. Does the source leave the observer with a definite judgment?

7. Does the source view the administration positively?

8. Do you like or dislike this information source? Why?

9. Having reviewed all this information for a month, how did it influence your view of the president and his administration?

Chapter 10

THE EXECUTIVE BRANCH AND POLICY IMPLEMENTATION

CHAPTER OUTLINE

Write a one-sentence summary of the materials found under each of the headings and subheadings in the text:

LEARNING OBJECTIVES

After reading Chapter 10 and doing the exercises in this study guide, you should be able to:

1. Explain the functions and organizational structure of the federal bureaucracy.
2. Understand the role of federal bureaucracies in regulating or deregulating the national economy.
3. Describe how civil service was created, how it was reformed, and how it currently functions.
4. Analyze what specific democratic controls can check the power of bureaucracies as political institutions.
5. Review the budget-making process and describe the three phases--preparational, congressional, and implementation.
6. Discuss the media's treatment of the bureaucracy.
7. List the basic merits and demerits of bureaucratic organization within the context of the American political system.

IDENTIFICATION ITEMS

Write out a one- or two-sentence identification that gives the significance of the following terms or names to this chapter:

Cabinet department
Independent regulatory commission
Department of the Interior
New regulation
Command and control regulation
Pendleton Act of 1883
Office of Personnel Management
Civil Service Reform Act of 1978
Trial balloon
Legislative oversight
Subgovernment
Executive reorganization
Budget time line
Budget and Impoundment Control
  Act of 1974
Entitlement program
Reconciliation
Sacred cow
Indexing
Grace Commission
Reduction in force tactic (RIF)

Max Weber
Bureaucracy
Independent agency
Bureau
Government corporation
Federal Reserve System
Capture theory
Old regulation
Incentive regulation
Hatch Act of 1939
Senior Executive Service (SES)
Whistleblowing
Legislative veto
Iron triangle
Congressional Budget Office
Impoundment
Uncontrollable expenditure
Tax expenditure
1986 Tax Reform Act
Oakland Project
Charles Schultze

REVIEW QUESTIONS

Multiple Choice Questions

1. A bureaucracy:
   a. is organized in a hierarchical fashion
   b. runs according to standardized procedures
   c. operates according to a division of labor
   d. all of the above

2. Which is true about the federal bureaucracy?
   a. Bureaucrats cannot be fired.
   b. The vast majority of bureaucrats do not work in Washington.
   c. Fewer than 1,000 bureaucrats are fired each year.
   d. The number of federal employees tripled from 1970 to 1980.

3. The federal government employs:
   a. 6 million people
   b. 4.8 million people
   c. 2.8 million people
   d. 5.6 million people

4. NASA is located in the:
   a. Defense Department
   b. State Department
   c. Interior Department
   d. none of the above

5. The independent regulatory agency which tests new drugs and medicines before they are marketed is the:
   a. FDA
   b. FCC
   c. SEC
   d. TVA

6. The first independent regulatory commission created by Congress was the:
   a. FTC
   b. ICC
   c. FCC
   d. OSHA

7. The capture theory meant that regulatory commissions:
   a. were strict regulators of industry
   b. became more than just symbols of regulation
   c. both a and b
   d. became weak regulators of industry

8. Which form of legislative oversight seeks to monitor policy implementation systematically, and which form seeks only to respond to complaints that arise about policy implementation?
   a. police patrol; fire alarm
   b. fire alarm; police patrol
   c. authorization; appropriation
   d. appropriation; authorization

9. The first industry to undergo deregulation in the late 1970s was the:
   a. airline industry
   b. trucking industry
   c. railroad industry
   d. broadcast industry

10. Charles Schultze favors a/an:
    a. command and control regulatory system
    b. incentive regulatory system
    c. totalitarian regulatory system
    d. democratic regulatory system

11. The civil service today:
    a. covers 90 percent of federal employees
    b. has most of its operations directed by the OPM
    c. both a and b
    d. has been eliminated by the Reagan administration

12. The GS for civil service jobs ranges from:
    a. 8 to 18   c. 1 to 18
    b. 1 to 12   d. 1 to 15

13. Under President Carter's 1978 Civil Service Reform Act:
    a. SES civil servants could receive bonuses for peak performance
    b. SES officials were frozen in their existing departments indefinitely
    c. The president lost his ability to move SES officials between agencies
    d. SES was abolished

14. The percentage of federal employees who are unionized is:
    a. 30   c. 25
    b. 80   d. 57

15. Which is not true about the legislative veto?
    a. By 1983, 200 statutes had legislative veto provisions.
    b. The legislative veto was struck down by the Supreme Court in 1983.
    c. The Supreme Court ruled that the veto was constitutional in 1983.
    d. All of the above are false.

16. The iron triangle is composed of:
    a. congressional committee members, cabinet members, and presidential advisers
    b. congressional committee members, agency officials, and lobbyists
    c. the three branches of government
    d. the president, Speaker of the House, and Chief Justice

17. Which is a tool of presidential control over the bureaucracy?
    a. presidential power to hire and fire
    b. authority to reorganize the executive branch
    c. both a and b
    d. none of the above

18. The Department of Education was created under the administration of President:
    a. Carter   c. Nixon
    b. Ford   d. Reagan

19. Social Security exemplifies a budgetary:
    a. sacred cow   c. both a and b
    b. uncontrollable item   d. tax expenditure

20. Secretary of Defense McNamara's experiment with the TFX plan demonstrated the effectiveness of:
    a. ZBB
    b. PPB
    c. indexing
    d. deficit financing

Completion Questions

1. Career employees of government agencies are termed _____.

2. Sixty-three percent of all federal employees are employed by the (number of) _____ cabinet departments.

3. The independent regulatory commission that oversees the nation's stock markets is the _____ and _____ Commission.

4. OSHA stands for _____ _____ _____ _____.

5. President Reagan ordered that _____ - _____ analysis be applied to bureaucratic rules and regulations.

6. The _____ Act of _____ established the federal civil service.

7. Collective bargaining among federal employees conflicts with the two civil service principles of the _____ system and _____ _____.

8. The two kinds of congressional committees that oversee federal agencies are _____ and _____ committees.

9. The key actor in the budget preparational phase is the _____.

10. _____ means that certain program benefits automatically rise in proportion to the rate of inflation.

True-False Questions

T   F   1. Max Weber was basically a pessimistic critic regarding bureaucracy's ability to solve national problems.

T   F   2. Bureaucratic growth has been greatest at state and local levels of government.

T   F   3. Each cabinet department is composed of many interrelated and interdependent bureaus, agencies, and services.

T   F   4. AMTRAK is a profitable government corporation.

T   F   5. New regulatory agencies were largely aimed at the general regulation of the economy.

T   F   6. When President Reagan took office, he revoked the reduction in force measures that had been imposed by President Carter.

T   F   7. Civil service employees are not allowed to make financial contributions to candidates.

T   F   8. The Plum Book refers to top-level political appointments.

T   F   9. The cumulative deficit of the federal budget from 1954 to 1983 totaled over a trillion dollars.

T   F   10. Less than one-quarter of the federal budget is uncontrollable.

Mastery Questions

Outline a response to each of the following:

1. Discuss the four aspects of the bureaucracy's relationship with the media.

2. What are the primary differences between the old and the new regulation?

3. Explain Charles Schultze's proposed incentive regulatory system and how it would differ from the existing system.

4. Explain the basics of civil service employment.

5. Review the budget timetable as set forth in the Budget and Impoundment Control Act of 1974. Cite the reasons behind the growing federal deficits.

6. List and explain bureaucratic strengths and weaknesses. Review the text's proposals for reform in the Viewpoint section.

ANSWERS TO REVIEW QUESTIONS (WITH PAGE NUMBERS)

Multiple Choice

1.	d, p. 300	11.	c, p. 312
2.	b, p. 300	12.	c, p. 311
3.	c, p. 301	13.	a, p. 312
4.	d, p. 302	14.	d, p. 312
5.	a, p. 306	15.	c, p. 314
6.	b, p. 305	16.	b, p. 315
7.	d, p. 307	17.	c, p. 314
8.	a, p. 307	18.	a, p. 316
9.	a, p. 308	19.	c, p. 322
10.	b, p. 310	20.	b, p. 323

Completion

1. bureaucrats, p. 299
2. thirteen, p. 302
3. Securities and Exchange, p. 306
4. Occupational, Safety and Health Administration, p. 307
5. cost-benefit, p. 309
6. Pendleton, 1883, p. 311
7. merit, affirmative action, p. 312
8. policy, appropriations, p. 313
9. OMB, p. 319
10. Indexing, p. 322

True-False

1. F, p. 300   6. F, p. 309
2. T, p. 303   7. F, p. 311
3. T, p. 303   8. T, p. 316
4. F, p. 305   9. T, p. 321
5. T, p. 307   10. F, p. 322

BEYOND THE TEXT: Making a Budget

Every year is a budget-making year, so you have an easily available resource in the nearest major university library for testing whether the generalizations discussed in the text are still valid. This exercise will acquaint you with three valuable sources of information about American government. These are The Budget of the United States for the most recent fiscal year, its companion document Special Analyses of the Budget, and the Statistical Abstract of The United States. These sources contain a mountain of information about American government and its activities. Use the index and table of contents to guide you to the pages that will enable you to answer the following questions:

1. How much money does the president plan to spend next fiscal year?

2. What is the percentage increase over previous years?

3. How large a deficit is planned?

4. Is this deficit consistent with the targets of Gramm-Rudman?

5. Are previous year expenditures consistent with the Gramm-Rudman targets for those years?

6. Looking at the pages that summarize federal expenditures by agency and by function, list the five categories slated to spend the most and the dollar amounts they are slated to spend:

Agency	Dollars	Function	Dollars

7. For each of the agencies indicated above, check the expenditures for previous years. Do the yearly increases conform to the incrementalism pattern discussed in the text? If not, can you discern any pattern in the increases? Speculate on why that pattern exists.

8. In the Special Analyses document, read the chapter on tax expenditures and list the ten categories with the largest dollar amounts.

Category   Dollars

_____   _____
_____   _____
_____   _____
_____   _____
_____   _____
_____   _____
_____   _____
_____   _____
_____   _____
_____   _____

9. Compare today's tax expenditures to those prior to the 1986 tax reform (prior
    to FY 1987). What changes have occurred after the 1986 tax reforms? Who in
    American society gets most of the benefits for each of these tax expenditures?
    (If the tax expenditures table in this year's Special Analyses do not go back
    prior to 1987, you can find that information by looking in the Statistical
    Abstract of the United States.)

Chapter 11

FEDERAL COURTS IN THE POLITICAL PROCESS

CHAPTER OUTLINE

Write a one-sentence summary of the materials found under each of the headings and subheadings in the text:

LEARNING OBJECTIVES

After reading Chapter 11 and doing the exercises in this study guide, you should be able to:

1. Define judicial review and distinguish between judicial activism and restraint. The significance of each (along with actual examples) should also be included.

2. Review the different historical periods of the evolution of the Supreme Court, noting key judicial developments and issues within each time frame.
3. Explain the procedures involved in Supreme Court and lower court appointments, noting the role of the president and Congress in the overall process.
4. Outline the federal court structure and the specific operations of the Supreme Court.
5. Discuss the importance of the litigation explosion to the federal courts.
6. Summarize the kinds of democratic controls on the court system, along with the general future of the court system in American politics.

IDENTIFICATION ITEMS

Write out a one- or two-sentence identification that gives the significance of the following terms or names to this chapter:

Roe v. Wade
Brown v. Board of Education
Criminal suit
Writ of mandamus
Judicial review
Statutory vs. fundamental law
Judicial activism
Age of laissez faire
Commerce clause
Due-process clause
Strict versus loose constructionism
Senatorial courtesy
Types of federal courts
Appellate jurisdiction
Dissenting opinion
Bakke case
National Court of Appeals plan
Alexis de Tocqueville
Warren Burger
Lewis Powell
Sandra Day O'Connor

Antonin Scalia
U.S. v. Nixon
Marbury v. Madison
Civil suit
Exclusionary rule
Judicial restraint
Court-packing plan
Dual court system
Original jurisdiction
Rule of four
Writ of certiorari
Concurring opinion
Dilemma of restraint
Oliver Wendell Holmes
Benjamin N. Cardozo
John Marshall
William Rehnquist
Harry F. Blackmun
John Paul Stevens
Judge W. Arthur Garrity

REVIEW QUESTIONS

Multiple Choice Questions

1. Legal disputes between individuals or organizations are termed:
   a. civil suits
   b. criminal suits
   c. judicial review disputes
   d. appellate suits

2. The Supreme invalidated a law of Congress for the first time in:
   a. McCulloch v. Maryland
   b. Marbury v. Madison
   c. Gibbons v. Ogden
   d. Roe v. Wade

3. A court order requiring an official to carry out a duty prescribed by law is a:
   a. writ of certiorari
   b. writ of habeas corpus
   c. writ of mandamus
   d. rule of four

4. Which of the following is true?
   a. The Burger Court is known for its judicial restraint.
   b. Justice Benjamin Cardozo was an advocate of judicial restraint.
   c. Justice Oliver Wendell Holmes was an advocate of judicial restraint.
   d. The Warren Court is known for its judicial restraint.

5. John Marshall was an advocate of:
   a. state supremacy over the federal government
   b. the belief that the U.S. Constitution was the creation of the people
   c. both a and b
   d. neither a nor b

6. The laissez-faire Supreme Court era is associated with this time period:
   a. 1801-1835
   b. 1953-1969
   c. 1865-1937
   d. 1969-1986

7. The National Industrial Recovery Act and the Agricultural Adjustment Act:
   a. expanded federal influence over the economy
   b. were ruled unconstitutional by the Supreme Court
   c. were key parts of the New Deal
   d. all of the above

8. Which of the following actions occurred under the Warren Court era?
   a. a broadening of the rights of the criminally accused
   b. an upholding of the 1964 Civil Rights Act
   c. both a and b
   d. neither a nor b

9. According to constitutional law scholars, the words that best describe the Burger Court are:
   a. confused and divided
   b. effective and intelligent
   c. below average
   d. activistic and liberal

10. What percentage of Supreme Court nominees are known by the president before he appoints them?
    a. 20 percent
    b. 40 percent
    c. 30 percent
    d. 60 percent

11. What is senatorial courtesy?
    a. the general cordiality between the president and the Senate on court appointments
    b. the custom that only senators may recommend names of possible Supreme Court nominees to the president
    c. the custom that any senator from the president's party can in practice veto a district court appointment in his or her state
    d. none of the above

12. Most Supreme Court justices have:
    a. had upper-class parents   c. worked for a major law firm
    b. attended a prestigious law school   d. all of the above

13. The Haynsworth and Carswell rejections occurred during the presidency of:
    a. Lyndon Johnson   c. Jimmy Carter
    b. Richard Nixon   d. John F. Kennedy

14. The Tax Court and the U.S. Court of Military Appeals are examples of:
    a. district courts   c. both state and federal courts
    b. special-purpose courts   d. federal courts of appeal

15. Which of the following is primarily a trial court?
    a. U.S. Court of Appeal   c. U.S. District Court
    b. U.S. Supreme Court   d. U.S. Adjutant General

16. One likely consequence of the types of judges President Reagan has appointed
    to the federal courts is:
    a. The courts will take a liberal direction.
    b. Liberal lawyers will bring more cases seeking judicial intervention on
        behalf of liberal social causes.
    c. Liberal lawyers will bring fewer cases seeking judicial intervention on
        behalf of liberal social causes.
    d. Conservative lawyers will bring more cases seeking judicial intervention
        on behalf of lower-class clients.

17. A Supreme Court order calling up a case for review is termed a:
    a. writ of certiorari   c. mandamus
    b. writ of four   d. note of standing to sue

18. A justice on the Supreme Court who votes with the majority but for different
    reasons is apt to write:
    a. a dissenting opinion   c. a concurring opinion
    b. a minority opinion   d. an opinion of the Court

19. Judge W. Arthur Garrity is associated with ordering desegregation of schools
    in:
    a. New York   c. Chicago
    b. Boston   d. Atlanta

20. To help the Supreme Court cope with its large case load, Chief Justice Burger
    urged:
    a. expansion of the Supreme Court to fifteen justices
    b. creation of a judicial ombudsman to screen cases for the Supreme Court
    c. creation of a National Appeals Court between the Supreme Court and the
        current Courts of Appeals
    d. a forty-eight-hour work week for justices so that they can do a better job
        of handling their cases

Completion Questions

1. In the Supreme Court ruling of _____ v. _____, state
   legislatures were prohibited from regulating abortions in the first trimester
   of pregnancy or outlawing them in the first six months of pregnancy.

2. As Alexander Hamilton argued in Federalist 78, the Constitution, which
   is _____ law, is superior to _____, as written by Congress.

3. "The final cause of the law is the welfare of society" is a statement
   attributed to Justice _____ _____.

4. The court-packing plan occurred under President _____ _____.

5. The Woodward and Armstrong book, _____ _____, described
   serious problems among members of the Burger Court.

6. Suits between citizens of different states are handled in _____
   courts.

7. The two kinds of jurisdiction are _____ and _____.

8. Warren Burger's successor as Chief Justice in 1986
   was _____ _____.

9. The Supreme Court finds itself restrained by _____,
   _____, _____.

10. Some observers argue that a _____ _____ of _____
    should be created to fit between the Supreme Court and the U.S. Courts of
    Appeal.

True-False Questions

T   F   1. In U.S. v. Nixon, the Supreme Court ruled that President Nixon had to
           release the Watergate tapes to the courts.

T   F   2. Judicial review is granted to the Supreme Court by Article III of the
           Constitution.

T   F   3. A living constitution that endures over time is an idea which is most
           compatible with judicial activism.

T   F   4. The commerce clause permits a sharing of interstate commerce between
           the national government and the states.

T   F   5. The Burger Court was a solidly conservative court.

T   F   6. Currently, there are nine U.S. District Courts.

T   F   7. President Reagan has tended to appoint conservatives to federal judgeships.

T   F   8. Federal judge nominees must be confirmed by a two-thirds majority vote of the Senate in order to receive their judgeships.

T   F   9. Federal judges are elected.

T   F   10. In the Viewpoint section, the text favors a period of greater judicial restraint.

Mastery Questions

Outline a response to each of the following:

1. Summarize the essential details and events surrounding the case of Marbury v. Madison.

2. Discuss the pros and cons of judicial restraint vs. judicial activism. Then show how Roe v. Wade was an example of judicial activism.

3. Review the four eras of Supreme Court history, explaining their significance in terms of judicial philosophy and/or constitutional history.

4. Explain how the president chooses men or women for positions on the Supreme Court.

5. Outline and explain the federal court structure.

6. What impact has the litigation explosion had on the federal courts?

ANSWERS TO REVIEW QUESTIONS (WITH PAGE NUMBERS)

Multiple Choice

1.	a, p. 337	11.	c, p. 352
2.	b, p. 339	12.	d, p. 352
3.	c, p. 339	13.	b, p. 353
4.	c, p. 341	14.	b, p. 354
5.	b, p. 344	15.	c, p. 355
6.	c, p. 344	16.	c, p. 353
7.	d, p. 347	17.	a, p. 356
8.	c, p. 348	18.	c, p. 358
9.	a, p. 351	19.	b, p. 359
10.	d, p. 351	20.	c, p. 360

Completion

1. Roe v. Wade, p. 337
2. fundamental, statutory, p. 339
3. Benjamin Cardozo, p. 342
4. Franklin Roosevelt, p. 347
5. The Brethren, p. 350
6. federal, p. 354
7. original, appellate, p. 354
8. William Rehnquist, p. 351
9. Congress, president, and public opinion, pp. 363-364
10. National Court of Appeals, p. 360

True-False

1. T, p. 338   6. F, p. 354
2. F, p. 339   7. T, p. 353
3. T, p. 341   8. F, p. 351
4. F, p. 346   9. F, p. 351
5. F, p. 349   10. T, p. 364

BEYOND THE TEXT: Writing a Brief of a Constitutional Law Case

This exercise is designed to give you some insight into how the Supreme Court
arrives at its conclusions and also to familiarize you with the major resource for
Supreme Court cases. Your resource is one of the three collections of Supreme
Court opinions: Supreme Court Reports, United States Reports, and Lawyers Edition
Reports. One of these collections will be either in your college library or in the
nearest law school library.

Your task here is to pick for review a contemporary Supreme Court decision. You
can use the text's appendix on important Supreme Court cases to choose a recent
case and to learn how to read the case citations. Or you can simply choose to
review a newer case that has been decided since this book was published. In either
instance, write a brief of no more than two single-spaced pages that includes the
following:

1. Name and citation of the case.

2. Facts of the case (one short paragraph)

3. Points of law the Supreme Court is being asked to decide (one sentence for
    each major point, in the form of a question)

4. The Court's decision on each point (stated, if possible, with a simple yes or
    no)

5. Opinion of the Court (one-paragraph summary of the reasons for the decisions)

6. Dissenting opinions (Give the names of the authors of each dissenting opinion
    and a one-sentence summary of each opinion.)

7. Concurring opinion (Give the names of the authors of each concurring opinion
    and a one-sentence summary of each opinion.)

Chapter 12

LIBERTY AND JUSTICE FOR ALL

CHAPTER OUTLINE

Write a one-sentence summary of the materials found under each of the headings and subheadings in the text.

LEARNING OBJECTIVES

After reading Chapter 12 and doing the exercises in this study guide, you should be able to:

1. Explain how the Bill of Rights was applied to the states as well as to the federal government.
2. Understand the constitutional development of the freedoms of speech, the press, assembly, and petition.
3. Discuss the constitutional background for current issues involving the freedom of religion, with special reference to establishment clause issues and free exercise issues.
4. Describe how a right to privacy has been created by Supreme Court rulings.
5. Outline the background of the civil rights struggle for racial minorities and the development of equal legal rights for women.
6. Assess the threat to constitutional liberties that exist today and are likely to exist in the American future.

IDENTIFICATION ITEMS

Write out a one- or two-sentence identification that gives the significance of the following terms or names to this chapter:

Bill of Rights
Freedom of expression
Bad-tendency test
Libel
Gag rule
Free-exercise clause
Exclusionary rule
Miranda rule
Right to counsel
Due-process clause
Separate-but-equal doctrine
Civil rights movement
Voting Rights Act of 1965
De facto segregation
Equal-protection clause
Freedom of Information Act
Foreign Intelligence Surveillance Court
Near v. Minnesota
Miller v. California
Engel v. Vitale
District of Abington v. Schempp
Gideon v. Wainwright
Miranda v. Arizona
Millikin v. Bradley
Swann v. Charlotte-Mecklenberg
  Board of Education
Committee for Public Education and
  Religious Liberty v. Nyquist
Alexander Hamilton
Thomas Jefferson

Thurgood Marshall
Martin Luther King
Incorporation
Clear-and-present danger test
Preferred-position test
Prior restraint
Shield law
Obscenity
Establishment clause
Moment of silence issue
Right to privacy
Double jeopardy
Jury trial
Cruel and unusual punishment
NAACP/LDF
Civil Rights Act of 1964
De jure segregation
Fourteenth Amendment
Gitlow v. New York
Schenck v. U.S.
Dennis v. U.S.
Yates v. U.S.
Roth v. U.S.
Mapp v. Ohio
Griswold v. Connecticut
Escobedo v. Illinois
Brown v. Board of Education
Earl Warren
Senator Joseph McCarthy

REVIEW QUESTIONS

Multiple Choice Questions

1. The founding father who felt a Bill of Rights was dangerous was:
   a. Thomas Jefferson   c. James Madison
   b. Alexander Hamilton   d. Thomas Paine

2. The prohibition against excessive bail or cruel and unusual punishment is found in the:
   a. First Amendment   c. Eighth Amendment
   b. Sixth Amendment   d. Ninth Amendment

3. The Supreme Court ruled in Barron v. Baltimore (1833) that:
   a. the Bill of Rights did apply to state governments
   b. the Bill of Rights did not apply to state governments
   c. states must not abridge the freedom of speech
   d. the Bill of Rights did not apply to any government

4. The Smith Act of 1940:
   a. was ruled unconstitutional by the Supreme Court
   b. made it illegal to advocate the violent overthrow of the United States government
   c. both a and b
   d. was resoundingly opposed by Senator Joseph McCarthy

5. Libel:
   a. does not apply to newspapers and what they print
   b. charges brought by public figures are relatively easy to prove in court
   c. applies only to spoken statements, not written ones
   d. applies to written or broadcast statements

6. Regarding the prohibition of obscene materials:
   a. the Supreme Court has precisely defined obscenity
   b. both Justices Black and Stewart have argued for prohibiting all materials
   c. obscenity is protected by freedom of speech
   d. obscenity, if proved, is not protected by freedom of speech

7. Most book-banning incidents involve:
   a. public schools
   b. public or community libraries
   c. professional writers and publishers
   d. research libraries

8. The NAACP Alabama case in 1958 dealt with:
   a. freedom of speech   c. freedom of religion
   b. freedom of the press   d. freedom of assembly and petition

9. Engel v. Vitale dealt with the issue of:
   a. school prayer   c. federal aid to education
   b. busing   d. pornography

10. The establishment clause is found in the:
    a. Fifth Amendment   c. Seventh Amendment
    b. Sixth Amendment   d. First Amendment

11. The test for separation of church and state includes:
    a. secular purpose
    b. no advocacy of religion
    c. avoidance of excessive church-state entanglement
    d. all of the above

12. To gain conscientious objector status, a person:
    a. must object to all wars
    b. must belong to an organized religion
    c. may object only to the particular war at issue
    d. must belong to an organized religion that rejects all war as immoral

13. The exclusionary rule is based upon the:
    a. First Amendment   c. Fifth Amendment
    b. Fourth Amendment   d. Sixth Amendment

14. Searches are considered reasonable:
    a. if a person consents to being searched
    b. if a warrant specifies the objects of the search
    c. both a and b
    d. if the police officer conducts the search before requesting a warrant

15. In Gideon v. Wainwright, the Warren Court ruled that:
    a. the accused could talk with a defense attorney during police interrogation
    b. states must provide lawyers to poor defendants in felony cases
    c. speedy trials were required by the Constitution
    d. all of the above

16. "You have the right to remain silent, and you have the right to talk to lawyer" are rights read to a suspect by police prior to interrogation. This practice is based upon the:
    a. Miranda decision   c. Mapp decision
    b. Escobedo decision   d. Gideon decision

17. During the Reagan administration, which of the following was an action taken by the administration that hindered civil liberties?
    a. The press was essentially blocked from covering the invasion of Grenada.
    b. The administration sought to censor publications of over 100,000 officials who had access to classified materials.
    c. The president issued an executive order that broadened the authority of government officials to withhold information from the public.
    d. All of these actions were taken by the Reagan administration.

18. The legislation that prohibited discrimination in public accommodations was the:
    a. Voting Rights Act of 1965   c. Civil Rights Act of 1964
    b. Equal Rights Act of 1954   d. Smith Act of 1940

19. The Supreme Court did not uphold a federal court ordered busing plan across school district boundaries in which case?
    a. The Swann ruling   c. The Gideon decision
    b. The Millikin decision   d. The Miranda warning

20. A major example of a witch hunt in American history was associated with:
    a. Ralph Nader   c. Senator Joseph McCarthy
    b. Martin Luther King   d. President Lyndon Johnson

Completion Questions

1. The amendment that protects the individual against unreasonable searches and seizures is the _____ Amendment.

2. _____ _____ means that you cannot be tried for the same crime twice if found innocent the first time.

3. The freedoms of expression include _____, _____, _____, and _____.

4. The landmark case that established the principle of no prior restraint was _____ v. _____.

5. _____ laws protect reporters from having to divulge confidential sources of information.

6. The _____ plan would give cash credits that parents could use to send their children to either a public or private school.

7. The first time the Supreme Court upheld the right of privacy was in _____ v. _____.

8. No one may be deprived of _____, _____, or _____ without due process of law.

9. Brown v. Board of Education reversed the separate-but-equal doctrine from the 1896 case of _____ v. _____.

10. Southern segregation was mainly _____ segregation; that is, required by law.

True-False Questions

T   F   1. Protection from double jeopardy and self-incrimination is found in the Fifth Amendment.

T   F   2. Schenck v. U.S. established the bad-tendency test regarding free speech.

T   F   3. The Supreme Court has extended First Amendment protection to cover symbolic speech.

T   F   4. The Supreme Court has not extended First Amendment protection to cover obscene materials.

T   F   5. According to the Supreme Court, local communities may place reasonable restrictions on where, when, and how a demonstration may be conducted.

T   F   6. It is constitutional for public funds to pay for secular textbooks for parochial school children.

T   F   7. The Boo Hoo Church was considered a legitimate religious organization by a federal court.

T   F   8. The Supreme Court has looked with favor upon the good-faith exception to the exclusionary rule.

T   F   9. The Supreme Court has ruled that the death penalty is cruel and unusual punishment.

T   F   10. An extensive attempt to implement comparable worth is being made in the State of Washington.

Mastery Questions

Outline a response to each of the following:

1. Review the evolution of Supreme Court thinking on applying the Bill of Rights to the states.

2. How has the Supreme Court ruled on free speech for advocates of unpopular causes and groups that are thought to be subversive?

3. Review the Supreme Court's position on financial aid to church-related schools; on prayer in public schools.

4. What are the arguments for and against a good-faith exception to the exclusionary rule?

5. Review the history of the Supreme Court's treatment of the death penalty.

6. How do new technology, private institutions, national security, and mass movements collectively constitute threats to civil liberties?

ANSWERS TO REVIEW QUESTIONS (WITH PAGE NUMBERS)

Multiple Choice

1. b, p. 371   6. d, p. 378
2. c, p. 373   7. a, p. 379
3. b, p. 372   8. d, p. 380
4. c, p. 375   9. a, p. 381
5. d, p. 376   10. d, p. 381

Multiple Choice

11.	d, p. 384	16.	a, p. 388
12.	a, p. 384	17.	d, p. 399
13.	b, p. 386	18.	c, p. 392
14.	c, p. 386	19.	b, p. 394
15.	b, p. 387	20.	c, p. 399

Completion

1. Fourth, p. 373
2. Double jeopardy, p. 373
3. speech, press, assembly, petition, p. 374
4. Near v. Minnesota, p. 376
5. Shield, p. 377
6. voucher, p. 384
7. Griswold v. Connecticut p. 385
8. life, liberty, property, p. 389
9. Plessy v. Ferguson, p. 392
10. de jure, p. 393

True-False

1.	T, p. 373	6.	T, p. 382
2.	F, p. 374	7.	F, p. 385
3.	T, p. 376	8.	T, p. 387
4.	T, p. 378	9.	F, p. 389
5.	T, p. 380	10.	T, p. 396

BEYOND THE TEXT: A Tolerance Test

Chapter 12 spends considerable space on the degree to which American citizens are committed to the First Amendment freedoms of religion, speech, press, assembly, and petition. The same issues were also raised earlier in Chapter 4, which suggested that college-educated people might be more committed to these freedoms than non-college-educated people and asked whether commitment to these freedoms has become stronger over time. The text also gave you the questions researchers use to probe the issue of tolerance in relation to freedom of expression. You can make an informal examination of how well the text's generalizations apply to people in your circles simply by raising these questions for discussion with them. Raise them with the old and the young, the college-educated and the non-college-educated, college freshmen and college seniors. Calculate the percent for each category of people you contact. How do your results conform to the expectations raised by the text? How do you respond to the test?

Person's Belief	Percent that would not allow this person to:	
	Teach in College	Give a Public Speech
doing away with elections and running the country through the military	_____	_____
atheism	_____	_____
Communism	_____	_____
antiblack racism	_____	_____
homosexual rights	_____	_____
belongs to a currently unpopular group that is resoundingly disliked by the person answering these questions	_____	_____

Chapter 13

FOREIGN AND DEFENSE POLICY

CHAPTER OUTLINE

Write a one-sentence summary of the materials found under each of the headings and subheadings in the text:

LEARNING OBJECTIVES

After reading Chapter 13 and doing the exercises in this study guide, you should be able to:

1. Trace America's development as a world power, stressing key historical events, the details of containment policy, and the Cold War period.
2. Identify those key institutions, agencies, groups, and individual leaders who collectively create U.S. foreign policy. Especially note the basic interaction between president and Congress on foreign policy.
3. Describe key foreign-defense policy challenges confronting the United States in the 1980s, such as NATO, trade, arms control, nuclear war, the Soviet threat, and terrorism.
4. Assess the strengths and weaknesses of the American foreign policy process.

IDENTIFICATION ITEMS

Write out a one- or two-sentence identification that gives the significance of the following terms or names to this chapter:

Third World
Manifest Destiny
Isolationism
Cold War
Containment policy
Marshall Plan
Detente
SALT I
Linkage
Congressional purse strings
War Powers Resolution of 1973
Intermestic issues
Interservice rivalries
CIA oversight
Massive retaliation
Triad of forces
Star Wars
Counterforce strategy
Flexible conventional response
George Kennan
Harry S Truman

Richard Nixon
League of Nations
Appeasement
Truman Doctrine
NATO
Cuban missile crisis
Nixon Doctrine
SALT II
Presidential primacy
Executive agreement
Major foreign policymaking
National Security Council
UDC
MAD strategy
MX
START talks
Strategic Defense Initiative
Nuclear proliferation
Quality v. quantity debate
George C. Marshall
Ronald Reagan

REVIEW QUESTIONS

Multiple Choice Questions
1. Historically, when did the United States step onto the broader world stage and begin to assert itself in world affairs?
    a. with the proclamation of the Monroe Doctrine
    b. during World War I
    c. during the Spanish-American War
    d. during the Civil War

2. Before Pearl Harbor, the percentage of the American public favoring armed resistance to Japan was:
   a. 19 percent
   b. 30 percent
   c. 9 percent
   d. 29 percent

3. The goal of supporting free people who are resisting subjugation by armed minorities or by outside pressure was enunciated by:
   a. George Kennan
   b. Harry Truman
   c. George C. Marshall
   d. Woodrow Wilson

4. How much economic aid was invested in Europe under the Marshall Plan?
   a. $2 billion
   b. $220 million
   c. $21 billion
   d. $12 billion

5. Which is true about the Cuban missile crisis?
   a. The Soviets withdrew their offensive missiles from Cuba.
   b. The U.S. pledged not to invade Cuba.
   c. Both a and b.
   d. Neither a nor b.

6. The Nixon Doctrine:
   a. advocated the use of U.S. troops to fight Communist insurrections in the Third World
   b. strove for military superiority over the Soviet Union
   c. both a and b
   d. neither a nor b

7. The policy of detente probably ended with the:
   a. Soviet cheating on SALT I
   b. Soviet actions in the city of Berlin
   c. Soviet invasion of Afghanistan
   d. Soviet attacks on China

8. Which is not a constitutionally granted foreign policy power of the president?
   a. commander-in-chief of the armed forces
   b. negotiation of treaties
   c. appointment of ambassadors
   d. declaration of war

9. Congressional checks on presidential foreign policy primacy include:
   a. the power of the purse
   b. Senate authority to reject treaties
   c. War Powers Resolution
   d. all of the above

10. Which factor will probably prevent Congress from taking a leading foreign policy role?
    a. dispersion of authority to many subcommittees
    b. the growth of congressional staff members
    c. weak party discipline
    d. intermestic issues

11. Whose administration announced that it would no longer abide by the nuclear arms limits of SALT II?
    a. Richard Nixon
    b. Ronald Reagan
    c. Gerald Ford
    d. Jimmy Carter

12. In the past, CIA covert activities have:
    a. been limited to foreign countries
    b. been conducted by the Intelligence Directorate
    c. both a and b
    d. none of the above

13. Which of the following is not a member of the National Security Council?
    a. secretary of defense
    b. vice president
    c. Senate majority leader
    d. CIA director

14. Public opinion:
    a. plays a major role in shaping U.S. foreign policy
    b. generally supports presidential initiatives in foreign policy
    c. is supportive throughout a long, inconclusive war
    d. has no effect at all on foreign policy

15. U.S. economic aid to foreign countries has been based upon:
    a. ensuring America's own economic status
    b. preventing unfriendly regimes from taking power
    c. humanitarian reasons
    d. all of the above

16. In comparison to the United States, Western Europe:
    a. is more eager to continue a detente with the Russians
    b. is more willing to strengthen NATO's deterrent capability
    c. both a and b
    d. is more eager for direct confrontation with the Soviet Union

17. MAD:
    a. was a military strategy preceding the doctrine of massive retaliation
    b. is based upon second-strike capabilities
    c. has clearly been accepted by Soviet strategists
    d. assumes that the United States will launch a first strike

18. The zero option plan:
    a. calls for zero ICBMs in Europe on both the U.S. and Soviet sides
    b. was first set forth by Soviet Premier Andropov
    c. calls for zero ICBMs except for those on submarines
    d. calls for zero reduction of all ICBMs

19. The Star Wars defense:
    a. could be developed in less than a decade
    b. would increase the possibility of a preemptive first strike
    c. has enjoyed universal support in the United States
    d. none of the above

20. Which is not a weakness of the U.S. foreign policy process?
    a. instability of top-level foreign policy personnel over time
    b. resilience of the U.S. political and economic systems
    c. disunity among foreign policymakers
    d. the tendency to seek military solutions to political problems

Completion Questions

1. Where World War I left a legacy of _____, World War II left one of opposition to _____.

2. The Soviet Union agreed to permit free elections in Eastern Europe at the _____ Conference in 1945.

3. NATO, standing for the _____ _____ _____ _____, was created in the year _____.

4. President Reagan's policy of _____ contained the idea that the Soviets would have to restrain their expansionism in various parts of the world in exchange for American cooperation and a policy of detente.

5. A formal understanding between the president and the chief executive of another nation-state is called an _____ _____.

6. The energy crisis and U.S. farm prices typify domestic-foreign policy links and hence are termed _____ issues.

7. The SALT I agreements prohibited installation of more than two _____ _____ _____ systems.

8. Brazil is an example of an LDC, or _____ _____ _____; India is a UDC, or _____ _____.

9. An ABM stands for _____ _____ _____.

10. According to the text, the cost of developing the Star Wars system technology could be between _____ billion and _____ billion dollars.

True-False Questions

T   F   1. Despite great political turmoil, the United States joined the League of Nations in 1923.

T   F   2. George Kennan argued that the containment policy could change Russian behavior over the long term.

T   F   3. Detente was a major element of the Nixon Doctrine.

T   F   4. The realist-conventional views are more acceptable to foreign policymakers than is revisionist theory.

T   F   5. American military forces have fought overseas over 125 times without a formal declaration of war.

T   F   6. The great bulk of intelligence gathering is gathered covertly by secret agents or spies.

T   F   7. Oversight of the Central Intelligence Agency has been tightened under the Reagan administration.

T   F   8. The economic growth rate of the LDCs is higher than that of the UDCs.

T   F   9. SALT II was never ratified by the United States Senate.

T   F 10. According to Paul Nitze, the Soviet Union rejects the MAD assumption of mutual deterrence.

Mastery Questions

Outline a response to each of the following:

1. How can you explain America's entrance into World War I as a combination of power politics and idealism?

2. What were the three major Cold War assumptions forming the basis of containment policy during the 1950s and 1960s? Were these assumptions correct or not? Differentiate between the realist and the idealist interpretations of the Cold War.

3. What constitutional and political factors enhance presidential primacy in the foreign affairs arena? What factors are likely to give Congress more influence over foreign policy in the future than it had at the height of the Cold War?

4. Does the rise of the national security adviser create more unity or conflict in the conduct of foreign policy?

5. Outline some of the political and economic challenges facing the United States from the LDCs and the UDCs.

6. What is the meaning of counterforce theory? Is it consistent with the MAD strategy?

7. What lessons can be learned from the F-5 vs. F-15, quality vs. quantity debate?

ANSWERS TO REVIEW QUESTIONS (WITH PAGE NUMBERS)

Multiple Choice

1.	c, p. 410	11.	b, p. 434
2.	a, p. 412	12.	d, p. 424
3.	b, p. 414	13.	c, p. 426
4.	d, p. 414	14.	b, p. 427
5.	c, p. 416	15.	d, p. 428
6.	d, p. 417	16.	a, p. 430
7.	c, p. 417	17.	b, p. 432
8.	d, p. 418	18.	a, p. 434
9.	d, p. 420	19.	d, p. 436
10.	a, p. 420	20.	b, p. 442

Completion

1. isolation; appeasement, p. 412
2. Yalta, p. 413
3. North Atlantic Treaty
   Organization, 1949, p. 414
4. linkage, p. 417
5. executive agreement, p. 420
6. intermestic, p. 421
7. anti-ballistic missile, p. 417
8. less developed country;
   underdeveloped country, p. 428
9. anti-ballistic missle, p. 430
10. 150 to 200, p. 436

True-False

1.	F, p. 411	6.	F, p. 424
2.	T, p. 415	7.	F, p. 425
3.	T, p. 417	8.	T, p. 428
4.	T, p. 418	9.	T, p. 433
5.	T, p. 418	10.	T, p. 437

BEYOND THE TEXT: Applying the War Powers Resolution

The Reagan administration has committed American military forces to action several times without previously asking the advice of Congress. These actions included the shooting down in 1982 of two Libyan military jets (after being fired on), the invasion of Grenada in 1983, the shelling by battleship in 1983 of one of the factions in the Lebanese civil war, the stationing of American Marines in Lebanon in 1983 and 1984, the forcing down in 1985 of an Egyptian airliner carrying terrorists who had hijacked a cruise ship and murdered an elderly American tourist, and the bombing of Tripoli, Libya, in 1986 following apparent Libyan involvement in the terrorist bombing of a West German night club in which some American servicemen were wounded and some killed.

Although most of these actions were immensely popular with the majority of Congress, the mainstream press, and the American public, in none of them did the administration ask for prior congressional approval. In some of the actions there was not even any prior consultation. In the action of the American Marines in Lebanon (which cost about 250 lives), the action extended far beyond the ninety-day period specified in the War Powers Resolution, without Congress either extending the period or ordering the Marines home. These actions raise several questions about the effectiveness of the War Powers Resolution, the legality of the president's acts, and the proper role of Congress in defense matters. What do you, as an educated citizen, think about the following?

1. Considering that some of these actions were possibly illegal under the terms of the War Powers Resolution, would a less popular president than Mr. Reagan face censure charges and possibly impeachment charges for violating the law? Depending on how you answered that question, what does your answer imply for the principle of law in defense policy? Is defense policy a matter of law or expediency?

2. Considering that the Supreme Court in 1983 struck down legislative vetoes, does the War Powers Resolution itself still have any legality? (It is a form of legislative veto, since it permits Congress by resolution to override presidential actions.) Given these considerations, is the president still bound by it?

3. Since the War Powers Resolution gives the president prior authority to engage in military actions for up to ninety days, does it have the effect of legitimizing in advance short-term military activities that might be illegal otherwise?

4. Despite the War Powers Resolution, Congress clearly had very little, if any, input into the military actions cited. Should Congress have greater input? If so, in what way should that input take place?

5. When the War Powers Resolution was passed in 1973, it had two main objectives: giving the president authority to use military force in crisis situations where American lives or property are threatened, and preventing the president from dragging the nation into another undeclared war such as the ones in Korea and Vietnam. Do you think that the current role of Congress in defense matters is strong enough to meet those objectives?

Chapter 14

THE POLITICS OF ECONOMIC AND SOCIAL POLICY

CHAPTER OUTLINE

Write a one-sentence summary of the materials found under each of the headings and subheadings in the text:

LEARNING OBJECTIVES

After reading Chapter 14 and doing the exercises in this study guide, you should be able to:

1. Explain the basic components of Keynesian economics and its influence upon the American political system, particularly in relation to the New Deal legacy.
2. Distinguish between fiscal and monetary policy and comment on the strengths and weaknesses of each.
3. Define supply-side economics and the basic assumptions underlying Reaganomics. In what sense is rational expectations theory an implicit criticism of Reaganomics? In what sense is it supportive of Reaganomics?
4. Understand the challenge of economic inequality in the United States and existing proposed policy remedies to the problems.
5. Describe the basics of social welfare policy and the challenge confronting it during the 1980s.
6. List and explain the characteristics of the political economy. Make specific reference to the federal government's managerial role, liberal-conservative differences, upper-status biases, indexing, and rational expectations theory.

IDENTIFICATION ITEMS

Write out a one- or two-sentence identification that gives the significance of the following terms or names to this chapter:

Capitalism
Social Darwinism
New Deal
Employment Act of 1946
Stagflation
Fiscal policy
Discount rate
Federal Reserve Board
International interdependence
Sunset vs. sunrise industries
Rising tide metaphor
Primary vs. secondary job market
Social insurance
Transfer payment program
In-kind assistance program
John Maynard Keynes
Milton Friedman
George Gilder
Ronald Reagan
Laissez-faire philosophy
Great Depression

Social Security Act of 1935
Great Society
Reaganomics
Monetary policy
Supply-side economics
Gramm-Rudman Plan
Rational expectations theory
Postindustrialization
Distribution of income
Zero-sum game
Poverty line
Cash assistance program
Entitlement program
Tax expenditure
Income maintenance plan
Horatio Alger
Lyndon B. Johnson
Lester Thurow
Charles Murray
Michael Harrington

REVIEW QUESTIONS

Multiple Choice Questions

1. Among the following industrialized countries, which one has the greatest
   degree of income inequality?
   a. West Germany   c. the United States
   b. Japan   d. France

2. The term that best characterizes the federal government's role during the
   nineteenth-century period of industrialization is:
   a. pure capitalism   c. laissez-faire
   b. pure socialism   d. Keynesian planning

3. The idea that a process of natural selection is at work in society as in
   nature was termed:
   a. populism   c. market economics
   b. Social Darwinism   d. evolutionary capitalism

4. A major economic management issue for the federal government in the middle
   1980s was:
   a. reinstituting Social Darwinism
   b. backing off from laissez-faire economics
   c. trying to inflate the economy
   d. reducing the federal budget deficit

5. The New Deal is associated with the presidency of:
   a. Herbert Hoover   c. Harry Truman
   b. Franklin D. Roosevelt   d. Calvin Coolidge

6. Which of the following seemed to confirm the effectiveness of Keynesianism?
   a. the deficit financing of the New Deal
   b. World War II massive deficit financing
   c. the budget reductions of Herbert Hoover in 1930
   d. the political economy of the late 1970s

7. The law passed in 1946 that made the Keynesian approach to economics
   government policy was the:
   a. Federal Mortgage Insurance Act
   b. Unemployment Compensation Act
   c. Savings Deposit Insurance Act
   d. Full Employment Act

8. Under President Lyndon B. Johnson, the official poverty rate fell from 25
   percent in 1960 to what percent in 1969?
   a. 9 percent   c. 12 percent
   b. 6 percent   d. 3.5 percent

9. Which of the following was not a key point of Reaganomics?
   a. deregulation   c. increasing taxes
   b. increased defense spending d. balancing the federal budget

10. Government regulation of interest rates and the money supply is termed:
    a. fiscal policy   c. financial policy
    b. monetary policy   d. supply-side policy

11. Which is _not_ a belief of supply-side economics?
    a. Tax and spending reductions are noninflationary.
    b. Unemployment would decrease while productivity would increase.
    c. Government revenues would be decreased by reducing income taxes.
    d. All of the above are beliefs of supply-side economics.

12. When the Federal Reserve Board raises bank reserves:
    a. economic activity is dampened
    b. economic activity is accelerated
    c. economic activity is unaffected
    d. economic activity is dampened and accelerated

13. Which U.S. industries have been the most competitive against foreign competition?
    a. automobile   c. steel
    b. service   d. electronic appliances

14. The notion that everybody's standard of living would improve as the economy grew was referred to in the text as the:
    a. zero-sum economy   c. supply-side economy
    b. growth increment   d. rising tide metaphor

15. The richest 15 percent of the population today earns about what share of all income in the nation?
    a. 38 percent   c. 18 percent
    b. 28 percent   d. 8 percent

16. Lyndon B. Johnson's Great Society sought to use the growth increment:
    a. to pay for social programs for the poor
    b. for wealthy investors initially
    c. in the same way as Lester Thurow
    d. for tax relief for all Americans

17. In 1984 the poverty line for a nonfarm family of four was just over:
    a. $6,000   c. $10,000
    b. $8,000   d. $12,000

18. The category of welfare benefits exemplified by Medicaid is referred to as:
    a. social insurance   c. in-kind assistance
    b. transfer payment   d. cash assistance

19. Which is true about Social Security?
    a. It is identical to private pension funds.
    b. Interfund borrowing appears to have solved the fiscal crisis of Social Security.
    c. It is the largest entitlement program.
    d. It is doomed to collapse by the year 2000.

20. COLAs:
   a. are a form of indexing   c. both a and b
   b. were pioneered by labor unions d. are irrelevant to the problem of
                                           inflation

Completion Questions

1. Free-market competition and private ownership of production characterize the
   economic system of _____.

2. The important New Deal program that originally provided pension supplements
   for the elderly was _____ _____.

3. Lyndon B. Johnson's War on Poverty was an integral part of
   his _____ _____ program.

4. High inflation and economic stagnation, occurring simultaneously, are
   collectively termed _____.

5. Monetary policy is the prime responsibility of
   the _____ _____ _____.

6. The most prominent monetarist is acclaimed
   economist _____ _____.

7. America's resource dependence is probably most dramatic in the case
   of _____ and _____.

8. Outmoded, unproductive, and inefficient U.S. industries,
   termed _____ industries, pose a major obstacle to
   reindustrialization.

9. If one takes into account the permanently poor, then about _____
   million Americans are poor nearly all the time.

10. Medicare and unemployment compensation are examples of _____
    programs that provide assistance to anyone who legally qualifies.

True-False Questions

T   F   1. The United States no longer leads the world in highest per capita GNP
            of all societies.

T   F   2. By the winter of 1932-33, U.S. unemployment reached 25 percent of the
            labor force.

T   F   3. Under the Lyndon Johnson administration, there was a dramatic
            reduction in the percentage of people living in poverty.

T   F   4. Under the Reagan administration, federal deficits have declined
            appreciably.

T F 5. Supply-side economists believe that supply will always create demand.

T F 6. The economic outlook of the poor under the Reagan program has grown worse, not better.

T F 7. Rational expectations theorists believe that the economy can be rationally managed very effectively.

T F 8. In a growing economy, the growth increment moderates somewhat the zero-sum nature of the economy.

T F 9. Charles Murray argues that the welfare programs of recent decades have made it harder rather than easier for people to escape poverty.

T F 10. In the hope of increasing the size of the labor force, labor unions have been advocating that corporations farm out work to people in their homes on a piecework basis.

Mastery Questions

Outline a response to each of the following:

1. What were the basic operating assumptions of the laissez-faire economic philosophy?

2. What were the important principles underlying Keynesian economics? Why did Keynesians not have an adequate response for the new economic conditions of the late 1970s?

3. What is supply-side economics? How did President Reagan attempt to implement its theories into actual policies? What were the basic successes and failures of Reagan's supply-side approach?

4. How has international interdependence affected the American economy? What are the positive and negative consequences of this development?

5. Describe the system of social welfare policy. How can social welfare programs be reformed?

ANSWERS TO REVIEW QUESTIONS (WITH PAGE NUMBERS)

Multiple Choice

1.	d, p. 450	11.	c, p. 457
2.	c, p. 450	12.	a, p. 460
3.	b, p. 451	13.	b, p. 464
4.	d, p. 455	14.	d, p. 467
5.	b, p. 452	15.	a, p. 465
6.	b, p. 453	16.	a, p. 467
7.	d, p. 453	17.	c, p. 468
8.	c, p. 455	18.	c, p. 472
9.	c, p. 456	19.	c, p. 473
10.	b, p. 456	20.	c, p. 479

Completion

1. capitalism, p. 450
2. Social Security, p. 452
3. Great Society, p. 454
4. stagflation, p. 455
5. Federal Reserve Board, p. 456
6. Milton Friedman, p. 459
7. petroleum; steel, p. 464
8. sunset industries, p. 464
9. 11 million, p. 469
10. entitlement, p. 471

True-False

1. T, p. 449	6. T, p. 459
2. T, p. 452	7. F, p. 461
3. T, p. 455	8. T, p. 466
4. F, p. 456	9. T, p. 467
5. T, p. 457	10. F, p. 481

BEYOND THE TEXT: Planning the National Economy

One way to gain some insight into the government's current economic policies and the main problems those policies address is to examine the current Economic Report of the President. This document is prepared each year by the Council of Economic Advisers and is usually published each February. To gain some broad insight into the government's perception of the state of the economy and its policies, read the president's message transmitting the report to Congress, and use the contents to locate tables that will enable you to answer the following questions:

1. What is the recent year's percentage change in the gross national product (GNP)?

2. How does this year's change compare with earlier years?

3. What is the recent year's change in inflation rate (as measured by the consumer price index or the GNP deflator)?

4. How does this year's change compare with previous years?

5. How high is the recent year's average unemployment rate? How does that compare with earlier years?

6. Examining the table that shows the GNP by industry, which industries appear to have the biggest share of the GNP? Comparing this year's results with twenty years ago, are there any changes? If so, how do those changes support or contradict some of the economic growth patterns discussed in the text?

7. After reading the president's transmittal address at the beginning of the report, what appear to be the president's three or four most serious economic concerns? How does he propose to deal with those concerns?

Chapter 15

EPILOGUE: WHAT NEEDS TO BE DONE?

CHAPTER OUTLINE

Write a one-sentence summary of the materials found under each of the headings and subheadings in the text:

LEARNING OBJECTIVES

After reading Chapter 15 and doing the exercises in this study guide, you should be able to:

1. Summarize the respective pros and cons of American political institutions.
2. List and discuss ten ways that the text claims will strengthen American politics.

IDENTIFICATION ITEMS

Write out a one- or two-sentence identification that gives the significance of the following terms or names to this chapter:

Fundamental rights
Representative democracy
Political stalemate
Oakland Project
New Towns in Town
Package legislation
Social Security reform
Philosophy of aggrandizement
Party decline
Marginally poor people
Single-issue politics
Strengths of the American political system

Weaknesses of the American political system
Checks and balances system
Executive emergency powers
Implementation problem
Model Cities program
Civil liberties
Political imagery-reality gap
ethic of restraint
Senator Joseph McCarthy
Dorothy Day Center
Limits of reform
Political participation

REVIEW QUESTIONS

Because of this chapter's special approach, only essay questions are presented here for review.

1. What are two basic reasons why it is difficult to discuss the strengths and weaknesses of American political institutions?

2. Review the four strengths of the American political system presented by the text. Think of current political developments. Do any of these have the capability of eroding the strength of the political system?

3. Review the five weaknesses of the American political system presented by the text. As in question 2, can you think of any current developments which may remedy any one or all of those weaknesses?

4. What factors have created a new class of marginally poor people?

5. Cite an example of a political reform which has had unforeseen and unintended consequences.

6. Why is it so important to the system of American government to increase political participation?

7. List the ten ways of improving American politics discussed in the text and write a short summary sentence after each of the ten recommendations. Include your opinion of the recommendation.